D1188757

Paris

France

EVERYMAN
CITY GUIDES

EVERYMAN CITY GUIDES
Copyright © 1998 David
Campbell Publishers, London

ISBN 1-85715-823-7

First published February 1998

Originally published in
France by Nouveaux Loisirs,
a subsidiary of Gallimard,
Paris 1997, and in Italy by
Touring Editore, Srl.,
Milano 1997
Copyright © 1997
Nouveaux Loisirs,
Touring Editore. Srl.

SERIES EDITOR
EDITORIAL MANAGER:
Seymourina Cruse
PARIS EDITION: Seymourina
Cruse, Sophie Lenormand
with Lionel Monéger
GRAPHICS
Élizabeth Cohat, Yann Le Duc
LAYOUT: Gérard Dumas,
Olivier Lauga, Yann Le Duc
AIRPORT MAPS
Kristoff Chemineau
MINI-MAPS, AROUND PARIS MAPS:
Édigraphie
STREET MAPS:
Touring Club Italiano
PRODUCTION
Catherine Bourrabier

Translated by Wendy Allatson

Edited and typeset by Book
Creation Services, London

Printed in Italy by
Editoriale Libraria

Authors and editors
PARIS

Things you need to know:
Lionel Monéger (1)
Historian Lionel Monéger has worked on
travel guides for Éditions Autrement and
Gallimard.

Where to stay: François Simon (2)
François Simon is a journalist who learned
his trade with the regional daily *Presse-
Océan* and *Gault Millau*. He has written
books on Paris hotels and restaurants and
was editor-in-chief of *Figaroscope* until 1997.

Where to eat:
Jean-Claude Ribaut (3)
Jean-Claude Ribaut has been writing the
gourmet column of the French national
newspaper *Le Monde* since 1989. He has
collaborated on several gourmet
publications and co-edited *Jardin des épices*
(Du May, 1992). His architectural training
and long-standing friendship with the French
chef, Jacques Manière, have helped to make
him an astute critic of gourmet cuisine.

After dark: Anne-Isabelle Jolly (4)
Anne-Isabelle Jolly is editor-in-chief of
several works on the theater, a frequent
contributor to the 'Sortir' column of
Femme magazine and presenter of a daily
theater review on French radio (FM 88.2).

What to see/Further afield:
René Maurice (5)
René Maurice is the author of several
historical works on Paris and the Île-de-
France and an enthusiast for the more
unusual aspects of Paris.

Where to shop:
Evelyne Vermorel (6)
Journalist Evelyne Vermorel writes for *Le
Point, Le Figaro* and *Vogue Homme* magazines.
In 1981, she founded the 'Beauté' column of
the *Madame Figaro* magazine and since 1994
has been director of international editions
of *Madame Figaro*, and contributing to the
Italian publication *Madame 'Class' Figaro*.

> *Note from the publisher:*
> *To keep the price of this guide as low as
> possible we decided on a common edition for
> the UK and US, which has meant
> American spelling.*

Contents

How to use this guide

This guide is divided into eight separate sections: **Everything you need to know** (information on travel and living in Paris); **Where to stay** (hotels); **Where to eat** (restaurants); **After dark** (going out); **What to see** (museum and monuments in the city); **Further afield** (places to visit around Paris); **Where to shop** (store guide); **Maps** (street maps and plan of the subway).

The **color** of the arrow box matches that of the corresponding dots on the mini-maps.

In the area gives you a feel for the location.

Basic facts

The most dazzling names in the jewelry w small but impressive area around the lege

The **area** (or the subject on a thematic page) is shown just above the map.
A map reference allows you to find places easily in the street map section.

Place Vendôme E A-B2

M Opéra

Shopping

Lise Rouge (35)
25 place Vendôme, 75001 ☎ 01 42 61 53 29

M Tuileries, Opéra **Men's and women's shirts and blouses** ☐ *(by appointment) Tue.–Sat. 10am–1pm, 2–6.30pm* ☐ *Duty-free for export, purchases mailed abroad*

The quality, precision and pleasure of made-to-measure shirts and blouses. Perfectly finished, with hand-embroidered monograms and Australian mother-of-pearl buttons, at surprisingly reasonable prices. The only problem experienced by its 1000 customers: which of the 1000 materials to choose.

Philippe Model (34)
33 place du Marché-Saint-Honoré, 75001 ☎ 01 42 96 89 02

M Tuileries, Pyramides **Hats, men's and women's footwear** ☐ *Tue.–Fri. 9am–7pm, Sat. 11–7pm* ☐ *Duty-free for export*

The season's creative designs are premiered at the spring race meetings, especially at Prix de Diane as worn by Chantal's magnificent... extravagant and variegated... the sophisticated but most elegant women. Designs for every pair... very restrained, and are presented alongside attractive ranges of footwear.

Maria Luisa (37)
2 rue Cambon, 75001 ☎ 01 47 03 96 15 ☎ 01 47 03 94 17

M Concorde **Women's wardrobe-peg fashion** ☐ *Mon.–Sat. 10.30am–7pm* ☐ *Duty-free for export*

This young Venezuelan uses personal taste and intuition to choose the very best of ready-to-wear fashion in French fashion design. Ranges include designs by Eric Bergère, as simple with a touch of humor and tiny checks for the finer figure.

Mayrovitz (28)
5 rue de Castiglione, 75001 ☎ 01 42 60 63 64 ☎ 01 42 61 34 30

M Tuileries **Opticians, optical instruments** ☐ *Mon.–Sat. 9.30–6pm* ☐ *Duty-free for export*

Alfonso XIII of Spain, Edward VIII of England and the Aga Khan are just three of the prestigious 'regulars' of Mayrovitz. Some styles are now available in exclusive gold and tortoiseshell designs. In the 1930s Mayrovitz produced a watch worn by both Charlie Chaplin as Charles Lindbergh. Today, it offers a wide range of binoculars, barometers and prescription spectacles, which are individually numbered, repaired and replaced in the event of theft, no matter where you are.

Not forgetting
■ **Dinh Van (39)** 18 rue de la Paix, 75002 ☎ 01 42 61 74 49 *Jewelry* ■ **Poiray (40)** 8 rue de la Paix, 75002 ☎ 01 42 61 70 58 *Jewelry* ■ **Daum (40)** 4 rue de la Paix, 75002 ☎ 01 42 61 25 25 *(table glass, decorative items)* ■ **Charvet (42)** 28 place Vendôme, 75001 ☎ 01 42 60 30 70 *Men's*

Not forgetting
■ **Dinh Van (39)** 18 r...
accessories ■ **Poiray (...)**
Jewelry ■ **Daum (41)** ...

Not forgetting lists places we also recommend, but don't have space to cover in full here.

M Tuileries, Opéra **Men's and women's shirts** ... appointment) Tue.–Sat. 10am–1pm, 2–6.30pm ... mailed abroad

Key information tells you what you ne to know about each particular place: the nearest underground station: the price rang accepted means of payment, and the variou services and facilities on offer.

The **opening page** of each
section gives an index of its
contents and some helpful hints.

Things you need to know
contains information on getting to
Paris and on travel and daily life in
the city.

Thematic pages
pick out a selection of
establishments linked by a
common element. These are
also shown on a simplified map.

Detailed **maps** are given in
the eighth section of the guide:
a map of the subway and
street maps.

Key

☎	telephone
➡	fax
●	price or price range
⏰	opening hours
▣	credit cards accepted
▣	credit cards not accepted
▼	toll-free number
@	e-mail address

Access

M	underground stations
P	parking
🅿	private parking
♿	facilities for the disabled
♿	no facilities for the disabled
🚆	train
🚗	car
⛴	boat
🚌	bus

Hotels

☎	telephone in room
📠	fax in room on request
🍸	minibar
📺	television in room
❄	air-conditioned rooms
🕐	24-hour room service
👥	caretaker
🧸	babysitting
➕	meeting room(s)
🐾	no pets
☕	breakfast
☕	open for tea/coffee
🍴	restaurant
🎵	live music
◉	club
🌳	garden, patio or terrace
🏋	gym, fitness club
🏊	swimming pool, sauna

Restaurants

🥗	vegetarian food
🏔	view
👔	smart dress required
🚬	smoking area
🍸	bar

Museums and galleries

🏪	on-site store(s)
📖	guided tours
☕	café

Stores

🔀	branches, outlets

Time difference
France is one hour ahead of Greenwich Mean Time (GMT). For example, when it is 6pm in Paris, it is 5pm in London and noon in New York.

Getting around

Electrical appliances
Electrical appliances in France operate on 220 volts and use 2-pin plugs ➡ 15.

Paris for all seasons
Spring: flowering chestnut trees and pleasant weather, but watch out for April showers!
Summer: pleasant weather (20°C, 67°F average), free parking in August.
Autumn: generally fine weather; the Paris trade fair season is at its peak in September.
Winter: low average temperatures (7–8°C, 46°F) but a full cultural calendar.

Changing money on arrival

Take French currency (French francs) with you if you are going to arrive in Paris late at night or if you don't want to waste time. The bureaux de change at Roissy and Orly airports are open daily from 6.30am–11.30pm, and in the mainline stations from 7–8am and 8–10.30pm. Alternatively, you can withdraw money from cash machines with an international credit card.

50
Things
you need to Know

Passport

EU nationals can stay in France for up to six months if they have a national identity card, and for an indefinite period if they have a valid passport. US and Canadian tourists visiting France for up to three months do not currently require a visa. Others should enquire about visa requirements before departure.

Health

EU nationals are covered for urgent medical treatment and should take form E111 with them ➡ 14. Non-EU nationals are not covered and are therefore advised to take out adequate medical insurance before departure.

Driving

Drivers must carry their driving license, car registration documents and certificate of insurance. The wearing of seat belts is compulsory on all roads.

▪ Departure lounge	▪ Check in	↗ TGV	✉ Post office
▪ Public area	▣ Bus	Ⓜ RER-Orlyval	🏢 Business center
▪ Airline desks	⊟ Taxis	🅷 Informations A	● Hotels
▪ Shops	▤ Car for hire	🔁 Bureau de Change	

➡ Getting there

Useful numbers

Flight times
☎ 01 36 68 15 15

Information
Orly
☎ 01 49 75 52 52
CDG
☎ 01 48 62 22 80

Police
Orly
☎ 01 49 75 43 04
CDG
☎ 01 48 62 31 22

Customs
Orly
☎ 01 49 75 84 00
CDG
☎ 01 48 62 35 35

Medical center
Orly
☎ 01 49 75 48 09
CDG Terminal I
☎ 01 48 62 28 00
CDG Terminal 2
☎ 01 48 62 53 32

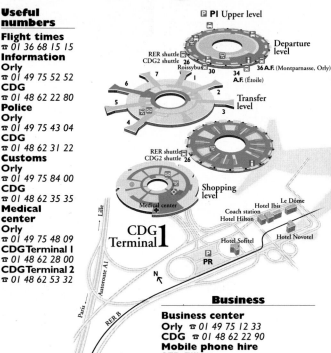

P PI Upper level

Departure level

RER shuttle
CDG2 shuttle 26
Roissybus 30 34 36 A.F. (Montparnasse, Orly)
7 1 A.F. (Étoile)
6 2
5 Transfer level
3
4

RER shuttle
CDG2 shuttle 26

Shopping level

Medical center

Hotel Ibis Le Dôme
Coach station
Hotel Hilton
Hotel Sofitel Hotel Novotel

CDG Terminal 1

P PR

N↖

Lille
Autoroute A1
Paris
RER B

Business

Business center
Orly ☎ 01 49 75 12 33
CDG ☎ 01 48 62 22 90
Mobile phone hire
SFR-Ellinas
☎ 01 48 16 10 99

Links from CDG

CDG to Paris
RER B
to *Gare du Nord & Chatelet-Les-Halles* (35–45 min)
📅 daily 4.55am–11.55pm ● F45
Taxi (45 min)
● F200 (approx.)
Bus Air France
to *Porte-Maillot & Étoile* (40 min)
📅 daily 5.40am–11pm ● F55
to *Montparnasse* (50 min)
📅 daily 7am–9pm

● F65
Roissybus to
Opéra (45 min)
📅 daily 5am–11pm ● F40

Roissy to Orly
RER B, Orlyval (70 min)
📅 Mon.–Sat. 6am–10.30pm; Sun. 7am–10.55pm ● F97
Taxi (60 min)
● F275 (approx.)
Bus Air France (50 min)
● F70

Links from Orly

Between west and south terminals
Orlyval (2 min) ● free

Orly to Paris
Orlyval
to *Châtelet* (35 min)
📅 Mon.–Sat. 6am–10.30pm; Sun. 7am–10.55pm ● F52
to *La Défense* (45 min)
● F62

Orlyrail
to *St-Michel* (35 min)
📅 daily 5.20–12.20am ● F35
Taxi (45 min)
● F145 (approx.)
Orlybus
to *Denfert-Rochereau* (25 min)
📅 daily 6am–11pm ● F30
Bus Air France
to *Invalides* (45 min)
daily 5.50am–11pm ● F40

Paris has two airports: Orly to the south and Roissy-Charles-de-Gaulle (CDG) to the north.

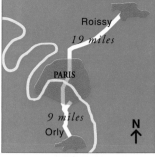

Roissy

19 miles

PARIS

9 miles
Orly

N

Hotels

At Roissy-CDG
Cocoon
☎ 01 48 62 06 16
➠ 01 49 19 77 78

Ibis
☎ 01 49 19 19 20
➠ 01 49 19 19 21

Novotel
☎ 01 48 62 00 53
➠ 01 48 62 00 11

Sofitel
☎ 01 49 19 29 29
➠ 01 49 19 29 00

Hilton
☎ 01 49 19 77 77
➠ 01 49 19 77 78

Sheraton

☎ 01 49 19 70 70
➠ 01 49 19 70 71

At Orly
Mercure
☎ 01 46 87 23 37
➠ 01 46 87 71 92

Hilton
☎ 01 45 12 45 12
➠ 01 45 12 45 00

Ibis
☎ 01 46 87 33 50
➠ 01 46 87 29 92

Aéroports de Paris

Rendezvous points

These are located near the Aéroports de Paris (ADP) desks.

Car rental

Avis
☎ 01 46 10 60 60
Budget
☎ 08 00 10 00 01
Citer-Eurodollar
☎ 01 44 38 61 61
Europcar
☎ 01 30 43 82 82
Eurorent
☎ 01 44 38 55 55
Hertz
☎ 01 39 38 38 38
Inter-touring Service
♿ Manual transmission
☎ 01 45 88 52 37

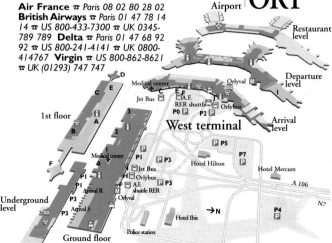

Paris Roissy Airport

CDG

RER B   TGV

D

N

P TGV
Sheraton

-A.F. (Etoile)

A.F.
P CD
(Montparnasse,
A.F.   Orly)
Roissybus
(Montparnasse,   Orly)
A.F. (Étoile)

P AB/G
Medical center

B

C

A

CDG
Terminal **2**   Transfer level

Arrival level

Airline companies

Air France ☎ Paris 08 02 80 28 02
British Airways ☎ Paris 01 47 78 14 14 ☎ US 800-433-7300 ☎ UK 0345-789 789 **Delta** ☎ Paris 01 47 68 92 92 ☎ US 800-241-4141 ☎ UK 0800-414767 **Virgin** ☎ US 800-862-8621 ☎ UK (01293) 747 747

Paris Orly Airport   # ORY

Restaurant level

Departure level

Arrival level

Medical center
Orlyval   M
E   F
Jet Bus   A.F.
RER shuttle   Orlyval
P0 P   P2 P   Orlybus

West terminal

D
C   E
1st floor
B   A
3
2

F

Medical center   P1
P1   P3
Jet Bus
Orlybus
P1   A.F.   P3
Arrival R   shuttle RER
Underground   M
level   Orlyval
P3
Arrival S

Ground floor

Police station

South terminal

P P5

P P7

Hotel Hilton

Hotel Mercure

A 106

N7

Hotel Ibis   →N

P P4

Basic facts

Paris, located in the center of western Europe, is also at the center of the French motorway and rail networks. TGV (1), Thalys (2) and Eurostar (3) trains travel from London, Amsterdam and Brussels to the Gare du Nord in Paris in record time. Paris has major parking problems

Getting there

By train

The city's six main-line stations are linked to the subway and bus networks. Métro map ➤ 172. Gare du Nord and Gare de Lyon are also linked to the RER (suburban express) network.

Main lines
There is one phone number for all the main-line stations. It deals with train times and ticket reservations.
☎ 08 36 35 35 35
Île-de-France Information:
☎ 01 53 90 20 20
Travelers with disabilities
☎ 08 00 15 47 53

Euraffaire

A business area and lounge is available for first-class passengers:
Gare Montparnasse
☎ 01 40 48 11 72
Gare de Lyon
☎ 01 53 33 16 56
Gare de l'Est
☎ 01 46 07 53 58

Stations

Gare du Nord
Services the northern French regions, the United Kingdom, Benelux countries and northern Germany.
Gare de l'Est
Services northeastern France, Switzerland, Austria and southern Germany.

Gare de Lyon
Services south-eastern France, Switzerland and Italy.
🍴 *Le Train Bleu*
➤ 66
Gare d'Austerlitz
Services central and southwestern France, Spain and Portugal.
Gare Montparnasse
Services western and southwestern France and Spain.
Gare Saint-Lazare
Services Normandy and the United Kingdom via the ports of Normandy.

Le Thalys

This high-speed

train operates a daily service between Belgium/the Netherlands and Paris.
Information/ reservations
☎ 08 36 35 35 36
Brussels–Paris
Gare de Bruxelles-Midi (Brussels) to Gare du Nord (Paris), 1hr 30 min (13 departures daily).
● *F580 roundtrip.*
Amsterdam– Paris
Amsterdam CS to Gare du Nord (Paris), 4 hrs 47 min (4 departures daily).
● *F798 roundtrip.*
Thalys Entreprises
☎ 01 47 16 27 37
🕐 *9am–6pm*

(5) and drivers are advised to use the city's parking lots (6).

Eurostar

Reservations
☎ UK 0990-300 003 or 0345 30 30 30 ☎ France 08 36 35 39
London–Paris
Eurostar high-speed train service between London (Waterloo Station) and Paris (Gare du Nord) via the Channel Tunnel in 3 hrs. Departures every hour during the week.
From London:
🕒 daily 5:08am–7:53pm
From Paris:
🕒 daily 6.37am–9:13pm
Lille–Paris
Gare de Lille-Europe to Gare du Nord (Paris)

in 2 hrs (departures hourly).
From Lille:
🕒 daily 7am–10pm
From Paris:
🕒 daily 7am–9pm

By bus

International buses to the Paris-Galliéni international bus station at Porte de Bagnolet.
Eurolines
Daily departures to Paris from major European cities.
☎ 01 49 72 51 51
🕒 8am–7pm

By car

Travel information
Drivers can obtain

information from the regional travel information center:
☎ 01 48 99 33 33
Information in French on short wave:
FIP 90.4 MHz during the day.
France Info 105.5 MHz in the evening.
Driving in Paris
There is a speed limit of 30mph (50kph) except on the *périphérique* (Paris ring road). Although driving in Paris does not present any particular problems, the same cannot be said for parking.
Parking
Pay and display Mon.–Fri., 9am–7pm

Charges vary according to districts.
● *F5–F15 per hour.* Tickets can be obtained from ticket machines using coins or parking cards available from tobacconists.
● *F100 and F200.*
Free parking Sundays and public holidays and throughout August.
Car pound It is quite common for cars to be towed away for obstruction. You can get the address of the local car pound from the nearest police station or the Préfecture de Paris.
☎ 01 53 71 53 53

Basic facts
Paris is served by a comprehensive public transport system. Buy a
'carnet' (book) of tickets for use on both the bus and metro systems.
On the bus you must stamp your ticket to validate it. Métro map ➡ 172.

Getting around

Public transport

The transport network is divided into 5 zones: 1 and 2 for the city of Paris, 3 to 5 for the suburbs. There is a standard fare for zones 1 and 2.
RATP Information
☎ 08 36 68 77 14
Tickets
RER (suburban express) and bus tickets available from ticket offices, machines in stations, and some tobacconists.
● F8 each; F46 for a book of ten.

Travel cards
'Carte Paris Visite'
Entitles you to unlimited journeys by subway, RER, bus and train within the Île-de-France (Paris region).
● 3/5 zones: F70/F170 (2 days); F105/F230 (3 days); F165/F315 (5 days)
'Formule 1'
One-day travel card
● 3 zones: F40; 1–5 zones: F100.

Métro
Map ➡ 172
With 15 lines and some 300 stations, the métro is the most compact subway network in the world. It has connections with the RER and SNCF (main-line) networks.
🕐 5.30–12.30am

RER
Map ➡ 172
Four suburban express lines (A, B, C, D) link Paris with the Île-de-France. Line C2 runs to Orly, C5 to Versailles and B3 to Roissy-Charles-de-Gaulle. Practical for quick trips across Paris.
🕐 5.30–12.30am

Bus
During the week, services operate on the 60 or so bus routes from 5.30am–8.30pm. Some run until 12.30am and on Sundays and public holidays. Few buses run after 1am.

Balabus
Runs between Arche de la Défense and Gare de Lyon (50 min).
🕐 7 Apr.–29 Sep.: Sun. and public holidays noon–8pm

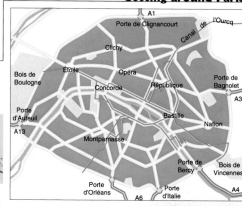

Batobus

The Batobus (boat-bus) offers a five-stop tour of the center of Paris (see map). It leaves from the Eiffel Tower (port de la Bourdonnais): *Musée d'Orsay* (Solférino); *Saint-Germain-des-Prés* (Quai Malaquais); *Notre-Dame* (Quai Montebello); *Hôtel de Ville* (town hall); *Louvre* (Quai du Louvre).

🚤 *May–June, Sep.: 10am–7pm; July–Aug.: 10am–9pm*
● *Inclusive: F60 (1 day); F90 (2 days);* F12 *per stop.*
☎ *01 44 11 33 44*

Taxis

Paris has 14,500 taxis. Unlike London and New York, taxis need not stop if hailed. Find one of the 460 taxi stands. A taxi is free when the Taxi sign is lit up, occupied when there is an orange light showing.

Charges

The pick-up charge is F13, and there is a surcharge for a fourth passenger or bulky luggage. Tips are not compulsory but it is customary to give 10%.

Complaints

In the event of difficulties, phone the Préfecture de Police:
☎ *01 45 31 14 80*

Taxi companies

Alpha Taxi
☎ *01 45 85 85 85*
Artaxi
☎ *01 42 41 50 50*
Taxis Bleu
☎ *01 49 36 10 10*
Taxi Étoile
☎ *01 42 70 41 41*
Taxi G7
☎ *01 47 39 47 39*

Cycling

Paris has 30 miles of cycle tracks, including two major cycle tracks: Bois de Vincennes to Bois de Boulogne, and Porte de Pantin to Porte de Vanves (see map). The quays along the Seine are for pedestrians and cyclists only on Sundays.

Cycle hire

● *F90 per day*
Paris à Vélo
9 rue Jacques-Cœur, 75004
☎ *01 48 87 60 01*
Paris Vélo
2 rue du Fer-à-Moulin, 75005
☎ *01 43 37 59 22*

The Office du Tourisme (1) on the Champs-Élysées will make reservations and provide information on events in Paris and the Île-de-France region. The Kiosque sells international newspapers, and there is a 24-hour bureau de change: Chèque Point. For lost property, go to the

➡ Getting by

Tourist Office

Office du Tourisme, 127 avenue des Champs-Élysées, 75008
☎ *01 49 52 53 54*
🕐 *9am–8pm*
Ⓜ *Charles-de-Gaulle-Étoile*

Money

Coins/notes
The French unit of currency is the franc (F). There are 100 centimes (cts) to the franc. Coins: cts5, 10, 20 and 50; F1, 2, 5, 10 and 20. Notes: F20, 50, 100, 200 and 500.
Exchange
To change cash, traveler's checks and Eurocheques you will need to present your passport or other proof of identity.

Banks
🕐 *Mon.–Fri. 9am–4.30pm. Most bureaux de change are open Sat. 9am–noon (some are open until 5pm).*
Approved bureaux de change
Chèque Point
150 avenue des Champs-Élysées, 75008
☎ *01 49 53 02 51*
🕐 *open 24 hours*
Thomas Cook
52 avenue des Champs-Élysées, 75008
☎ *01 42 89 80 32*
🕐 *8.30am–11pm*
Bank transfers
American Express
11 rue Scribe, 75009
☎ *01 47 14 50 00*
🕐 *9am–6.30pm*

Press

Dailies
Le Monde; Le Figaro; Libération; *Le Parisien.*
Weeklies
L'Événement du Jeudi; Le Nouvel Observateur; Le Point; L'Express.
International press kiosk
Corner of the avenue Matignon and the Champs-Élysées, 75008
🕐 *open 24 hours*

English-language bookstores

Paris has a number of centrally-located English-language bookstores.
Brentano's
37 avenue de l'Opéra, 75002
☎ *01 42 61 52 50*
Galignani
224 rue de Rivoli, 75001
☎ *01 42 60 76 07*
W. H. Smith
248 rue de Rivoli, 75001
☎ *01 44 77 88 99*

Phone calls

Phone numbers
To phone abroad from Paris, dial 00 followed by the national code (e.g. Australia 61; Great Britain 44; New Zealand 64; USA and Canada 1) followed by the number you are calling.
Public phones
Most public call boxes take phone cards, which are available from France Télécom agencies, tobacconists and RATP ticket offices.
Information
National: *12*
International: *00 33 12* + national no.

Objets Trouvés (2), and the Poste du Louvre (3) is open all night if you have urgent mail to send.

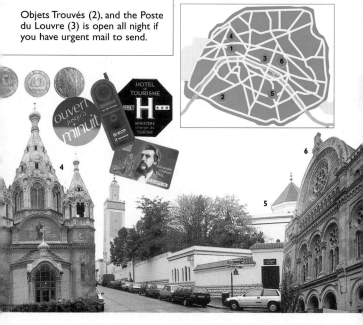

Mail

Main post office
52 rue du Louvre, 75001
🕐 *open 24 hours*
☎ *01 40 28 20 00*

Express mail
Chronopost
7 rue Hérold, 75001
☎ *01 45 21 64 00*
🕐 *Mon.–Fri. 8am–7.45pm; Sat. 8am–1pm.*

DHL
59 avenue d'Iéna, 75016
☎ *01 45 01 91 00*
🕐 *Mon.–Fri. 9am–7.45pm; Sat. 9am–4.45pm.*

Religious services

Catholic
Notre-Dame
Île de la Cité, 75004
☎ *01 43 26 07 39*

Protestant
Oratoire du Louvre
145 rue Saint-Honoré, 75001
☎ *01 42 60 21 64*

Orthodox
Saint-Alexandre-de-la-Neva
12 rue Daru, 75008
☎ *01 42 27 37 34*

Jewish
Synagogue Nazareth
15 rue Notre-Dame-de-Nazareth, 75003
☎ *01 42 78 30 10*

Muslim
Grande Mosquée de Paris
place du Puits-de-l'Ermite, 75005
☎ *01 43 31 38 20*

Electrical appliances

These operate on 220V. For information on adapters and transformers:

BHV
52-64 rue de Rivoli, 75001
🕐 *Mon.–Tue., Thur.–Fri. 9.30am–7pm; Wed. 9.30am–10pm.*

FNAC
Forum des Halles, 75001
🕐 *Mon.–Sat. 10am–7.25pm*

Emergencies

Emergency medical service ☎ *15*
Police ☎ *17*
Fire service ☎ *18*
Medical emergency ☎ *01 43 37 77 77*
Dental emergency ☎ *01 43 37 51 00*
Anti-poison Center ☎ *01 40 37 04 04*
Ambulances ☎ *01 43 78 26 26*
Pharmacy
Derhy
84 avenue des Champs- Élysées, 75008
☎ *01 45 62 02 41*
🕐 *daily, open 24 hours*
Ⓜ *F. - Roosevelt*

Lost property

Possessions
Objets trouvés
36 rue des Morillons, 75015
☎ *01 55 76 20 20*
🕐 *Mon., Wed., Fri. 8.30am–5pm; Tues., Thur. 8.30am–8pm.*

Credit cards
If your credit card is lost or stolen, contact:
Visa
☎ *01 42 77 11 90*
Eurocard
☎ *01 45 67 53 53*

Passports
Register the loss or theft of your passport immediately at the nearest police station and your national embassy.

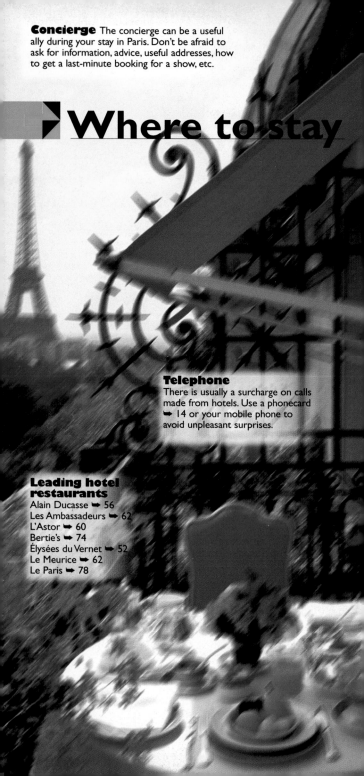

Concierge The concierge can be a useful ally during your stay in Paris. Don't be afraid to ask for information, advice, useful addresses, how to get a last-minute booking for a show, etc.

Where to stay

Telephone
There is usually a surcharge on calls made from hotels. Use a phonecard ➡ 14 or your mobile phone to avoid unpleasant surprises.

Leading hotel restaurants
Alain Ducasse ➡ 56
Les Ambassadeurs ➡ 62
L'Astor ➡ 60
Bertie's ➡ 74
Élysées du Vernet ➡ 52
Le Meurice ➡ 62
Le Paris ➡ 78

Hotel prices

Hotel prices are listed net, but there may be a surcharge for pets, cots, breakfast, etc. If the hotel has a private car park, compare charges with those of the nearest public parking lots. The price of accommodation may be negotiable out of season and when there are no major Paris exhibitions, trade fairs or conferences.

Hotels

THE INSIDER'S FAVORITES

Vacating your room

Rooms are usually vacated by 11.30am. After a long stay, most managers are more flexible and may even offer to keep your luggage until the evening. However, they are perfectly within their rights to charge you for half a day.

Twelve avenues converge on the place Charles de Gaulle, known as l'Étoile (the star), with the Arc de Triomphe at its center. This area combines quiet residential districts and busy avenues full of restaurants and luxury shops. ■ Where to eat ➡ 52 ➡ 54 ➡ 74 ■ After dark

Where to stay

Hôtel Mercédès (1)
128 avenue de Wagram, 75017 ☎ 01 42 27 77 82 ➡ 01 40 53 09 89

Ⓜ *Wagram* 🅿 *35 rooms* ●● *2 suites F850* 🅥 *F50* ▢ ◉ ▣ ⌷ ⌷ ⌷ 🅈 🅵

The Hôtel Mercédès comes as a pleasant surprise in the Étoile district. Its furniture and general design are in 1930s style with occasional authentic details such as the Gruber windows. The private rooms are decorated in pastel shades and there is one spectacular split-level suite (no. 720).

Hôtel Pergolèse (2)
3 rue Pergolèse, 75016 ☎ 01 40 67 96 77 ➡ 01 45 00 12 11

Ⓜ *Argentine* 🅿 *40 rooms* ●●● 🅥 *F65* ▢ ◉ ▣ ▣ ⌷ ⌷ *safe* 🅈 🆇 🅇

The Pergolèse is designed in resolutely contemporary style by Rena Dumas. It opts for elegance in its choice of materials (leather, white marble, oak) and names (MacConnico and Stark). A delightfully restful interior.

Libertel Hôtel d'Argentine (3)
1 rue d'Argentine, 75116 ☎ 01 45 02 76 76 ➡ 01 45 02 76 00

Ⓜ *Argentine* 🅿 *40 rooms* ●● 🅥 *F75* ▢ ◉ *7am–11pm* ▣ ▣ ⌷ ⌷ *safe* 🅈 🆇 🅇

Situated in a quiet, narrow street, only a stone's throw from the Arc de Triomphe and the Champs-Élysées, the Hôtel d'Argentine offers the comfort of a private residence and personal, friendly service. The designer, F. Méniche, took great care with the refurbishment of this neoclassical residence. The mahogany furniture and commemorative plaque, presented by the ambassador of Argentina, may well be an attempt to escape from the more traditional Empire style, with extensive use of imitation marble and Greek-style plaster. The private rooms echo the same themes on a more modest scale, while bathrooms are luxuriously marbled.

Hôtel Raphaël (4)
17 avenue Kléber, 75016 ☎ 01 44 28 00 88 ➡ 01 45 01 21 50

Ⓜ *Kléber* 🅿 🕅 *90 rooms* ●●●●● *35 suites F3900* 🅥 *F120* ▢ ◉ ▣ ▣
⌷ ⌷ 🍴 *Dining room* 🅈 *Bar* ➡ *86* 🝖 🆇 🅇 ✚ ✦ 🔰

Among the leading Paris hotels on account of its unique atmosphere, and the studied authenticity of its Louis XV decor, Persian carpets and stylish elegance. A chic, well-groomed clientele adds to its typically Parisian charm. The luxurious private rooms offer extensive views across Paris. Dine in the restaurant to complete the experience.

Not forgetting
■ **Hôtel Étoile-Péreire (5)** 146 boulevard Péreire, 75017
☎ 01 42 67 60 00 ➡ 01 42 67 01 90 ●● ■ **Hôtel Élysée Ceramic (6)**
34 avenue de Wagram, 75008 ☎ 01 42 27 20 30 ➡ 01 46 22 95 83 ●●

➠ 86 ➠ 88 ➠ 100
■ What to see
➠ 106

Close to the place Charles de Gaulle-Étoile, the façade of the Élysée Ceramic (1904) is an example of Parisian art nouveau.

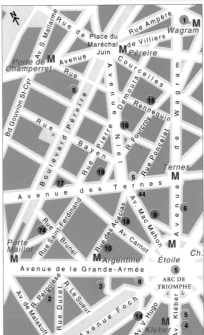

6

2

2

ETOILE PEREIRE
HÔTEL ★★★

4

5

This largely residential, wealthy area contains some of the city's finest restaurants as well as the Musée Marmottan and the Musée Guimet. ■ Where to eat ➡ 56 ➡ 74 ■ What to see ➡ 106 ■ After dark ➡ 90

▶ Where to stay

Hôtel Baltimore (7)
88bis avenue Kléber, 75016 ☎ 01 44 34 54 54 ➡ 01 44 34 54 44

Ⓜ *Boissière* Ⓟ 🄝 *104 rooms* ●●●●● *1 suite F3500* 🄦 *F135* ▱ ◐
▱ ☎ Ⅲ▸ 🄵▸ Ⅲ 🄵🄵 *Le Bertie's* ➡ 74 ⓨ *Le Copper Bar* ▨ 🄴🄴 🄴 *reception rooms* 🄴🄴 🄴 @ *baltimore@cie.fr*

Built in 1892, the hotel claims to have been at least partly designed by Gustave Eiffel. The impressive dimensions of its particularly spectacular entrance are enhanced by marble and by elaborate architectural decoration. The same theme is echoed less ostentatiously in its private rooms, where the emphasis is on modern comfort (the hotel was restored in 1991).

Le Parc Victor Hugo (8)
55–57 avenue Raymond-Poincaré, 75016
☎ 01 44 05 66 66 ➡ 01 44 05 66 00

Ⓜ *Victor-Hugo, Trocadéro* Ⓟ 🄝 *120 rooms* ●●●●● *20 suites F2950*
🄦 *F135* ▱ ◐ ▱ ☎ Ⅲ▸ 🄵▸ *safe* 🄵🄵 *Alain Ducasse* ➡ 56, *Le Relais du Parc*
ⓨ ▨ 🄴🄴 🄴 🄵 🄴🄴 🄴 🄥 *0800 908 567*

One of the most successful modern luxury hotels in recent years. It occupies a former mansion (1912) and offers an exceptional menu under the direction of the master chef, Alain Ducasse. The rooms have been designed by top names (Nina Campbell, David Linley) with an eye to the type of comfort befitting one of the best Paris hotels. A clientele consisting of the international elite and the gourmet jet set.

K. Palace (9)
81 avenue Kléber, 75016 ☎ 01 44 05 75 75 ➡ 01 44 05 74 74

Ⓜ *Trocadéro* Ⓟ *83 rooms* ●●●● *15 suites F2610* 🄦 *F105* ▱ ◐
▱ ☎ Ⅲ▸ 🄵▸ Ⅲ 🄵🄵 *Le Carré Kléber* ⓨ 🄵 *reception rooms* ▧ 🄴🄴
@ *Kpalace@Wanadoo.fr*

This 1990s luxury hotel was designed by Ricardo Bofill. Its modern decor combines leather and chrome enhanced by blond wood. It is no surprise then that its rooms are often reserved by fashion magazines so that top models can pose in a sophisticated modern setting.

Hôtel Massenet (10)
5bis rue Massenet, 75116 ☎ 01 45 24 43 03 ➡ 01 45 24 41 39

Ⓜ *Passy* Ⓟ *41 rooms* ●● 🄦 *F40* ▱ ▱ ☎ 🄵▸ ⓨ 🄴🄴 🄴 🄵

A family residence converted into a delightful hotel. A successful combination of Louis XV furnishings, modern decor and tradition (the Mathieu family has been running the hotel for three generations). The Massenet offers some spectacular views, including that of the familiar outline of the Eiffel Tower visible from the terrace.

Not forgetting
■ **Hôtel Garden Élysées (11)** 12 rue Saint-Didier, 75116
☎ 01 47 55 01 11 ➡ 01 47 27 79 24 ●●●●

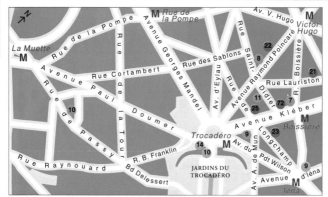

The quiet, flower-filled gardens of
the Parc Victor Hugo are an ideal setting in which to
enjoy the cuisine of the Relais du Parc.

Despite large investment and some improvement, the famous broad avenue of the Champs Élysées, lined with shops and restaurants, has not altogether recovered the charm and elegance of the 19th century.
■ Where to eat ➡ 48 ➡ 52 ➡ 56 ➡ 60 ➡ 66 ➡ 74 ■ After dark

▶ Where to stay

Hôtel Vigny (12)
9–11 rue Balzac, 75008 ☎ 01 40 75 04 39 ➡ 01 42 99 80 40

Ⓜ *George-V* 🏇 *37 rooms* ●●●●● *11 suites F2600* 🔄 *F90* ▦
⏱ ▦ 🛎 🎬 🛗 🍴 🎭 🔲 🍸 🍽

Only a stone's throw from the Champs-Élysée, this hotel, listed by Relais et Châteaux, is a haven of peace and quiet. It combines charm and excellence with decor designed by Nina Campbell in 19th-century English style (antiques, four-poster beds).

Hôtel Vernet (13)
25 rue Vernet, 75008 ☎ 01 44 31 98 00 ➡ 01 44 31 85 69

Ⓜ *Charles-de-Gaulle-Étoile* 🅿 🏇 *57 rooms* ●●●●● *3 suites F3700*
🔄 *F120* ▦ ⏱ ▦ 🛎 🎬 🛗 🍴 🎭 🍽 *Élysées du Vernet* ➡ *52* 🍸 🍽 🎾 🍽 ✚

A small, old-fashioned hotel located in a quiet street off the Champs-Élysées, with its excellent cuisine served in an exquisite dining room with an Edwardian glass roof. Open fires in its bar and lounges and live piano music make afternoon tea or an aperitif very appealing. The comfortable private rooms are decorated in neoclassical style. Peace, elegance and excellent service.

Plaza-Athénée (14)
25 avenue Montaigne, 75008 ☎ 01 53 67 66 65 ➡ 01 53 67 66 66

Ⓜ *Alma-Marceau* 🅿 🏇 *205 rooms* ●●●●● *42 suites F4900* 🔄 *F160* ▦ ⏱
▦ 🛎 🎬 🛗 🍴 🎭 *in the suites* 🍽 *Le Régence, Relais Plaza* 🍸 🍽 🎾 🍽 ✚
reception rooms 🎀 *hairdresser* ❇ 🌿 🔽 *0800 136 136*

This exceptional hotel is situated in the heart of the haute couture and jewelry district of Paris. Opened in 1897 and still considered one of the best hotels in the world, it boasts Louis XV, Louis XVI and Regency furniture and a highly-sophisticated international clientele. Excellent cuisine and a very pleasant patio garden.

San Regis (15)
12 rue Jean-Goujon, 78008 ☎ 01 44 95 16 16 ➡ 01 45 61 05 48

Ⓜ *Franklin-Roosevelt, Champs-Élysées* 🅿 🏇 *34 rooms* ●●●●●
10 suites F3200 🔄 *F110* ▦ ⏱ ▦ 🛎 🎬 🛗 🍴 🎭 🔲 🍸 🎾 🏊 🌿 🍽 🌿 @
hotel-sanregis.fr

A former 18th-century mansion with a magnificent neoclassical façade. Its very 'English' decor is a blend of Empire, Chippendale, Regency and Queen Elizabeth, while it is furnished in 17th- and 18th-century style. It has a lounge opening onto a winter garden and a lovely restaurant. The suites with balconies enjoy a superb view of Paris and the Eiffel Tower.

Not forgetting

■ **Bradford Élysées (16)** 10 rue Saint-Philippe-du-Roule, 75008
☎ 01 45 63 20 20 ➡ 01 45 63 20 07 ●●
■ **Châteaubriand (17)** 6 rue d'Artois, 75008
☎ 01 40 76 00 50 ➡ 01 40 76 09 22 ●●●●

➡ 86 ➡ 92 ➡ 96
■ What to see ➡
106 ■ Where to
shop ➡ 142 ➡ 144

Luxury settings – wood paneling,
gilt and stylish furniture – reflect
the aristocratic elegance of the
so-called 'Golden Triangle'.

SAN REGIS

The Place de la Concorde lies between the Louvre and the Arc de Triomphe, like a clearing in the Parisian landscape. It offers some splendid views of the city and is within easy reach of a number of museums.
■ Where to eat ➥ 62 ➥ 66 ➥ 74 ■ What to see ➥ 104

▶ Where to stay

Le Crillon (18)
10 place de la Concorde, 75008 ☎ 01 44 71 15 00 ➥ 01 44 71 15 02

Ⓜ *Concorde* 🅿 🛎 *120 rooms* ●●●●● *43 suites F4900* 📺 *F165* ▤ ◑ ▣
☎ ⅲ 🛗 🎋 *Les Ambassadeurs* ➥ 62, *L'Obélisque* 🎵 📺 💠 🎾 🏂 ✚ 💱 ⊞

Le Crillon, the most majestic of the luxury hotels in Paris, is located in one of the world's most beautiful squares. It occupies an 18th-century palace and boasts an exquisite gold and marble façade. The rooms and suites are elegant and spacious, and some – such as the Leonard Bernstein suite overlooking place de la Concorde – are truly exceptional. Anticipate or prolong the experience by sampling the cuisine of Dominique Bouchet in Les Ambassadeurs restaurant.

Hôtel Costes (19)
239 rue Saint-Honoré, 75001 ☎ 01 42 44 50 00 ➥ 01 42 44 50 01

Ⓜ *Tuileries* 🅿 🛎 *85 rooms* ●●●●● *4 suites F3000* 📺 *F100* ▤ ◑ ▣ ☎
ⅲ 🎋 *Café Coste* 📺 🏂 〰

Beyond the main courtyard lies a small Italian-style *palazzo*. Jean-Louis Costes called upon interior designer Jacques Garcia to create the hotel of his dreams. Garcia mixed styles, superimposed periods and combined the classic with the extravagant. The result is both stunning and familiar. Spacious rooms and unique decor make this a truly delightful place to stay.

Lotti (20)
7 rue de Castiglione, 75001 ☎ 01 42 60 37 34 ➥ 01 40 15 93 56

Ⓜ *Tuileries* 🅿 🛎 *131 rooms* ●●●●● *2 suites F4900* 📺 *F120* ▤ ◑ *7am–midnight* ▣ ☎ 🛗 ⅲ 🎋 *Le Lotti* 📺 💠 🎾 🏂 🏂 ✚ 📺 *0800 258 021*

The smallest of the grand hotels has preserved its early 20th-century club atmosphere, where members were only accepted on recommendation. The tradition has been maintained and now celebrities such as Paul McCartney, Paul Newman and Jane Fonda enjoy its discreet and personal service.

Hôtel Meurice (21)
228 rue de Rivoli, 75001 ☎ 01 44 58 10 10 ➥ 01 44 58 10 78

Ⓜ *Tuileries* 🅿 🛎 *180 rooms* ●●●●● *30 suites F3900* 📺 *F150* ▤ ◑ ▣ ☎
ⅲ 🎋 ⅲ 🎋 *Le Meurice* ➥ 62 📺 💠 🎾 🏂 🏂 ✚ *reception rooms*

The Meurice, designed at the turn of the century, became known as the *Hôtel des Rois* (Hotel of Kings) for its regal welcome. Its magnificent marble interior sparkles with chandeliers, and is furnished with antiques, sculptures and old master paintings. Part of the hotel's appeal is that, for all its tradition and elegance, the service is attentive and friendly.

Not forgetting
■ **Grand Hôtel Intercontinental (22)** 3 rue de Castiglione, 75001
☎ 01 44 77 11 11 ➥ 01 44 77 14 60 ●●●●●
■ **Royal Saint-Honoré (23)** 221 rue Saint-Honoré, 75001
☎ 01 42 60 32 79 ➥ 01 42 60 47 44 ●●●●

■ Where to shop ➥
i46 ➥ 150

The Hôtel Meurice offers guests a unique view of the Jardin des Tuileries and the Eiffel Tower while they enjoy a traditional breakfast.

Place de la Madeleine, famous for its bustling flower market since 1834, is a pleasant place to stay. Situated in a continually changing district, it has become one of the gourmet centers of Paris and boasts specialist delicatessens, and some of the city's top restaurants.

▶ Where to stay

Concortel (24)
19–21 rue Pasquier, 75008 ☎ 01 42 65 45 44 ➠ 01 42 65 18 33

Ⓜ *Madeleine, Saint-Augustin* Ⓟ *46 rooms* ●● *12 suites F810* 🗇 *F45* ▭ Ⓞ
▭ 🗇 🗂 ⅲ ⅲ ⅲ ⅲ 🗳 ⚹

The Concortel occupies a 19th-century building conveniently located near the district's main department stores. Decorated in a combination of ancient and modern styles, it provides a high level of modern comfort and attracts a regular clientele who appreciate its location. Attentive and discreet service and a quiet, flower-filled garden are two of its key strengths.

Westin Demeure Hôtel Astor (25)
11 rue d'Astorg, 75008 ☎ 01 42 66 56 56 ➠ 01 53 05 05 30

Ⓜ *Saint-Augustin, Madeleine* Ⓟ 🗇 *134 rooms* ●●●●● *5 suites F2950*
🗇 *F135* ▭ Ⓞ ▭ 🗇 🗂 ⅲ 🗇 *L'Astor* ➠ *60* ⅲ 🗇 🗳 🗇 🗇

This newly built hotel has attracted attention not only for the very real comfort of its brand new premises (classic 1930s decor) but also for a menu that marks the unexpected comeback of Joël Robuchon. The famous chef is acting only in a consultative capacity, but a corner of the menu is reserved for his best-known dishes, including the famous purée that gourmets thought had disappeared forever. Rooms at higher levels offer a spectacular view of Paris.

Hôtel Beau Manoir (26)
6 rue de l'Arcarde, 75008 ☎ 01 42 66 03 07 ➠ 01 42 68 03 00

Ⓜ *Madeleine* Ⓟ *29 rooms* ●●● *3 suites F1350* 🗇 *included* ▭ Ⓞ ▭ 🗇 ⅲ
🗂 ⅲ 🗳 @ *beaumanoir@wanadoo.fr*

The Hôtel Beau Manoir, already extremely pleasant before it was renovated, has since moved up the league table of the district's top hotels. The 18th-century decor includes wood paneling, handmade walnut furniture, Burgundy stone and beautiful Aubusson tapestries. Coordinated cotton prints, sofas, wing chairs, and Moustier earthenware lamps add to the sophistication of its spacious private rooms, most of which have their own lounge area. A calm and elegant place to stay.

Alison (27)
21 rue de Surène, 75008 ☎ 01 42 65 54 00 ➠ 01 42 65 08 17

Ⓜ *Madeleine* Ⓟ *35 rooms* ●● 🗇 *F45* ▭ ▭ 🗇 🗂 🗳 🗇

This recently renovated hotel occupies a 19th-century building in a busy part of the district. Its clientele reflects its location, which is ideal for business people and tourists alike. It has a small central courtyard and offers practical, modern comfort in a surprisingly peaceful setting.

Not forgetting

■ **Lido Hôtel (28)** 4 passage de la Madeleine, 75008 ☎ 01 42 66 27 37
➠ 01 42 66 61 23 ●●●

Madeleine **E** A1-2

■ Where to eat ➡ 60 ➡ 62
■ Where to shop ➡ 140
➡ 148

A sophisticated breakfast in a sophisticated setting: the Hôtel Beau Manoir.

27

Since the end of the 19th century, place Vendôme has been considered the most successful expression of classical architecture in Paris. It provides a beautiful setting for world-famous jewelers', the major fashion houses and the city's luxury hotels.

Where to stay

Ritz (29)

15 place Vendôme, 75001 ☎ 01 43 16 30 30 ➡ 01 43 16 31 78

Opéra P 187 rooms ●●●●● 45 suites F4700 F180
L'Espadon Vendôme, Hemingway
reception rooms beauty salon Ritz Club

Since it opened in June 1898, the Ritz has been the very epitome of luxury. The first Paris hotel to have electricity, it enjoys a unique location in elegant place Vendôme. Mohammed Al-Fayed, who bought the hotel in 1979, has ensured that the Ritz both retains its traditions (including splendid afternoon tea) and offers modern facilities such as a fitness center and swimming pool. Fabulous restaurant.

Hôtel Castille (30)

37 rue Cambon, 75001 ☎ 01 44 58 44 58 ➡ 01 44 58 44 00

Opéra P 107 rooms ●●●●● 8 suites F3200 F135
safe Il Cortile reception rooms

The Hôtel Castille stands next to the famous fashion house of Coco Chanel in what was once the Ritz Annex. Its style is both Parisian (decor by Jacques Grange in 20 of its rooms) and Venetian, with 87 rooms graced with marble, engraved glass, painted wood furniture and lamps. Ask for one of the rooms that overlook the beautiful central courtyard with its sculpted fountain.

Westminster (31)

13 rue de la Paix, 75002 ☎ 01 42 61 57 46 ➡ 01 42 60 30 66

Opéra P 102 rooms ●●●●● 18 suites F3600 F110
safe Le Céladon Les Chenets reception rooms
0800 463 441 @ sales@westminster.hepta.fr

Two hundred years ago, the Westminster was a convent. During the reign of Napoleon III, it was a post house. In 1900, it was given a stone façade and, in 1981, it was bought by the Warwick chain. Today, this luxury English-style hotel offers modern comfort and convenience in period surroundings. All rooms are regularly redecorated. Guests can enjoy an aperitif in the intimate atmosphere of the hotel's bar and the excellent cuisine of its restaurant: Le Céladon.

Hôtel Mansart (32)

5 rue des Capucines, 75001 ☎ 01 42 61 50 28 ➡ 01 49 27 97 44

Opéra P 51 rooms ●● 6 suites F1200 F50

This former private residence is located 'next door' to the Ritz, on the corner of the place Vendôme and the rue des Capucines. It enjoys a privileged position and a unique view, especially from the Suite Mansart. The rest of the hotel is a successful blend of classic – Regency and Baroque – styles.

■ After dark ➡ 88 ➡ 90 ➡ 82 ■
Where to shop ➡ 150

29

30

The hotels in the vicinity of place Vendôme combine traditional elegance with the facilities of modern luxury hotels.

29

31

Where to stay

Hôtel Régina (33)
2 place des Pyramides, 75001 ☎ 01 42 60 31 10 ➡ 01 40 15 95 16

Ⓜ *Tuileries, Pyramides* ℗ *130 rooms* ●●●●● *14 suites F2700* 🅦 *F95* ▭ ◐ ▣ ▣ ⠿ ⫙ ⫶ ⓨ ⬥ ⊠ ⌖ ⌕ ✚ *reception rooms* 〜

Movie directors often choose to film against the backdrop of this Second-Empire hotel, with its vast entrance hall and lounges pervaded by the scent of wax polish. Its *fin de siècle* atmosphere is enhanced by its art nouveau decor and Louis XV- and Louis XVI-style furniture. An English bar and a restaurant with a beautiful open fireplace (1900) add a pleasantly cozy touch. Last and by no means least, the Régina is located in the heart of historic Paris and enjoys spectacular views of the Louvre ➡ 104 and the Jardin des Tuileries ➡ 122.

Louvre Saint-Honoré (34)
141 rue Saint-Honoré, 75001 ☎ 01 42 96 23 23 ➡ 01 42 96 21 61

Ⓜ *Louvre, Palais-Royal* ℗ *40 rooms* ● 🅦 *F45* ▭ ▣ ▣ ⫙ *safe* ⫶ ⓨ

The Louvre Saint-Honoré combines classic (in its private rooms) and modern (in its public rooms) styles. In the modern vein, a glass pyramid links the hotel's two buildings. It is ideally located for shopping: near Les Halles and only a stone's throw from the rue Montorgueil and its famous market, and the designer boutiques of the place des Victoires ➡ 154.

Tonic Hôtel (35)
12–14 rue du Roule, 75001 ☎ 01 42 33 00 71 ➡ 01 40 26 06 86

Ⓜ *Châtelet* ℗ *34 rooms* ●● *1 suite F950* 🅦 *F35* ▭ ◐ ▣ ▣ ⫙ ⫶ ⓨ

One of the main advantages of this modern hotel is undoubtedly its location: between the church of Saint-Eustache, Les Halles and rue de Rivoli, and very close to the Louvre. Functional rooms, some of which have been recently renovated with jacuzzis and saunas.

Hôtel de la place du Louvre (36)
21 rue des Prêtres-Saint-Germain-l'Auxerrois, 75001 ☎ 01 42 33 78 68 ➡ 01 42 33 09 95

Ⓜ *Louvre, Rivoli, Pont-Neuf* ℗ *20 rooms* ●● *2 split-level suites F812* 🅦 *F50* ▭ ◐ ▣ ▣ ⫙ ⓨ ⬥ 〜 @ *123France.com/hotlouv.htm*

This old building was successfully renovated in 1989. The vaulted breakfast room, known as the *Salle des Mousquetaires* (Musketeers' Room), used to be linked to the Louvre. A key attraction is its spectacular view of the colonnaded façade of the Louvre and the church of Saint-Germain-de-l'Auxerrois, the parish church of the French kings.

Not forgetting
■ **Tuileries (37)** 10 rue Sainte-Hyacinthe, 75001 ☎ 01 42 61 04 17 ➡ 01 49 27 91 56 ●●●
■ **Relais du Louvre (38)** 19 rue des Prêtres-Saint-Germain-de-l'Auxerrois, 75001 ☎ 01 40 41 96 42 ➡ 01 40 41 96 44 ●●●

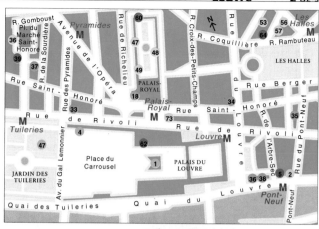

The staircase in the Tuileries, the building once the residence of Marie Antoinette's first lady-in-waiting.

33

33

36

The Marais district lies on the north bank of the Seine near the Île Saint-Louis. One of the most historic districts of Paris, its charm is heightened by its many small squares and gardens. ■ Where to eat ➡ 72 ■ After dark ➡ 92 ■ What to see ➡ 110 ■ Where to shop ➡ 160

Where to stay

Pavillon de la Reine (39)
28 place des Vosges, 75003 ☎ 01 40 29 19 19 ➡ 01 40 29 19 20

Ⓜ *Saint-Paul, Bastille* Ⓟ 🅟 **55 rooms** ●●●●● *20 suites F2200* 🅥 *F95* ▣ ⓪
▣ 🅢 🅛 Ⅲ 🅧 🅧

Set back from the place des Vosges, built by Henri IV in 1609, and close to Musée Carnavalet, the Pavillon de la Reine is one of the most delightful hotels in Paris. Liberty prints and beautiful stonework create an atmosphere of great charm.

Pavillon Bastille (40)
65 rue de Lyon, 75012 ☎ 01 43 43 65 65 ➡ 01 43 43 96 52

Ⓜ *Bastille* Ⓟ **24 rooms** ●● *1 suite F1200* 🅥 *F65* ▣ ⓪ ▣ 🅢 🅛 Ⅲ 🅧
🅧 🅝 @ *hotel-pavillon@akMail.com*

Opened in 1991, the Pavillon Bastille is favored by singers from the nearby Opéra-Bastille. Its discreet, muted atmosphere combines magnificent modern decor – by Jean-Pierre Heim – with the soft yellows and blues of the private rooms. A delightful flower-filled patio with an 18th-century fountain.

Hôtel des Deux Îles (41)
59 rue St-Louis-en-l'Île, 75004 ☎ 01 43 26 13 35 ➡ 01 43 29 60 25

Ⓜ *Pont-Marie, Cité* Ⓟ **17 rooms** ●● 🅥 *F47* ▣ ⓪ *7am–8pm* ▣ 🅢 *safe* Ⅲ
🅧 🅧 🅧

A 17th-century building with unusual decor: wooden blinds, cane chairs, bamboo furniture painted blue and yellow, a cellar-bar with an open fireplace and a flower-filled patio with a murmuring fountain.

Hôtel du Jeu de Paume (42)
54 rue St-Louis-en-l'Île, 75004 ☎ 01 43 26 14 18 ➡ 01 40 46 02 76

Ⓜ *Pont-Marie* Ⓟ **32 rooms** ●●● 🅥 *F80* ▣ ⓪ ▣ 🅢 🅛 🅨 🅦 🅧 🅧 🅧
➕ 🅧 🅧 ★

This leading hotel stands on the site of the royal-tennis court (1634) which was converted into a private mansion. It has a particularly skilful blend of contemporary and 17th-century styles, and the sophisticated elegance of its atmosphere is enhanced by the fabrics of Pierre Frey ➡ 148, exposed beams and limed oak. Most rooms overlook the small patio and well-lit garden.

Not forgetting

■ **Hôtel Saint-Merry (43)** *78 rue de la Verrerie, 75004 ☎ 01 42 78 14 15*
➡ *01 40 29 06 82* ●●●
■ **Hôtel Saint-Paul-le-Marais (44)** *8 rue de Sévigné, 75004*
☎ *01 48 04 97 27 ➡ 01 48 87 37 04* ●
■ **Hôtel de Lutèce (45)** *65 rue Saint-Louis-en-l'Île, 75004*
☎ *01 43 26 23 52 ➡ 01 43 29 60 25* ●●

44

40

42

42

40

42

The 17th- and 18th-century buildings of the Marais and Île St-Louis contrast with the modern architecture of the Bastille district.

le pavillon BASTILLE

43

42

The Latin Quarter is the district of the famous Paris universities (*Sorbonne*, *Beaux Arts*, *Sciences Politiques*) where the young student population combine the serious business of study with enjoyment and relaxation. ■ Where to eat ➡ 76

▶ Where to stay

Relais Hôtel Vieux Paris (46)
9 rue Gît-le-Cœur, 75006 ☎ 01 44 32 15 90 ➡ 01 43 26 00 15

Ⓜ *Saint-Michel* Ⓟ *13 rooms* ●●● *7 suites F1370* 🏨 *F70* ▭ ⓪ ▣ ☎ ⌷ ▥ 🍴 ⌷ ☒ 🚭 🌿 @ *vieuxpar@worldnet.fr*

This beautiful Directory-style hotel occupies a timbered, freestone building dating from 1480. Its more recent guests have included members of the beat generation – Allen Ginsberg, William Burroughs, Jack Kerouac – who have all sat on the flower-filled terrace overlooking the roofs of Paris and the Sainte-Chapelle.

Hôtel Esméralda (47)
4 rue St-Julien-le-Pauvre, 75005 ☎ 01 43 54 19 20 ➡ 01 40 51 00 68

Ⓜ *Saint-Michel* Ⓟ *19 rooms* ● 🏨 *free for residents* ▭ ⓪ ☎ 🌿

Sophia Loren has often stayed in this small hotel opposite Notre-Dame. The beams and old stone of the 17th-century building combine with art nouveau decor to create the blend of bohemian and Vieux Paris styles appreciated by its regular clientele. Don't miss the tiny church of St Julien-le-Pauvre (rebuilt 1165) in square Viviani, which has the oldest tree in Paris, a false acacia planted in 1620.

Relais Médicis (48)
23 rue Racine, 75006 ☎ 01 43 26 00 60 ➡ 01 40 46 83 39

Ⓜ *Saint-Michel* Ⓟ *16 rooms* ●●● 🏨 *free for residents* ▭ ⓪ *6.30am–7pm* ▣ ☎ ⌷ ▥ *safe* ⊠ ☒

A consistently popular style of hotel. It uses all the tricks of the trade and combines all the latest fashions in contemporary decoration and design: Italy, Provence, mixed marble floors and smart fabrics. The overall effect is skilfully managed, giving a cheerful and bright atmosphere that ensures the success of this 18th-century hotel.

Select Hôtel (49)
1 place de la Sorbonne, 75005 ☎ 01 46 34 14 80 ➡ 01 46 34 51 79

Ⓜ *Cluny* Ⓟ *68 rooms* ●● *1 split-level suite F1250* 🏨 *F30* ▭ ⓪ ▣ ☎ ▥
Ⓨ ☒ 🌿

The Select Hôtel has the unique advantage of being the only hotel on the medieval place de la Sorbonne. This is reinforced by the successful combination of contemporary decor with beams and stone walls, a fountain in the entrance hall and a unique view of the Sacré-Coeur ➡ 112, and the Tour Saint-Jacques.

Not forgetting

■ **Les Rives de Notre-Dame (50)** 15 quai Saint-Michel, 75005
☎ 01 43 54 81 16 ➡ 01 43 26 27 09 ●●●
■ **Hôtel Luxembourg (51)** 4 rue de Vaugirard, 75006
☎ 01 43 25 35 90 ➡ 01 43 26 60 84 ●●

■ After dark ➥ 90 ■ What to see ➥ 120

49

Not far from the Jardin du Luxembourg, fountains murmur in the entrance halls and gardens of the hotels of the *Quartier latin*.

46

48

HOTEL
*Les Rives
De
Notre-Dame*

47

The Left Bank is famous for its literary and cultural circles. The universities and the Panthéon remain, but less studious visitors may prefer to visit the Jardin du Luxembourg ➡ 122. ■ After dark ➡ 98 ■ What to see ➡ 120 ➡ 122

Where to stay

Hôtel des Jardins du Luxembourg (52)
5 impasse Royer-Collard, 75005 ☎ 01 40 46 08 88 ➡ 01 40 46 02 28

Ⓜ *Luxembourg* Ⓟ *25 rooms* ●● Ⓥ *F50* 🔲 🔳 📷 🛗 Ⅲ *safe* 🍸 🚭

There is an atmosphere of studied elegance in this quiet hotel, designed by Haussmann in one of the city's old cul-de-sacs, only a stone's throw from the Jardin du Luxembourg ➡ 122. Its decor pays attention to detail – oak floor, kilims and mahogany furniture – in a sophisticated combination of the contemporary and the exotic. The small but elegant private rooms are extremely comfortable. Freud stayed here on his first visit to France.

Hôtel des Grands Hommes (53)
17 place du Panthéon, 75005 ☎ 01 46 34 19 60 ➡ 01 43 26 67 32

Ⓜ *Luxembourg* Ⓟ *32 rooms* ●● *2 suites F870* Ⓥ *F45* 🔲 🔳 📷 🛗 Ⅲ 🍸 🚭 ✚ 🌿

During the 1930s, this 18th-century hotel was popular with such Surrealist writers and artists as Breton and Soupault. Today, they are remembered in a contemplative and friendly atmosphere. All the rooms are decorated with different fabrics, and English furniture abounds. The attic rooms are particularly delightful and offer a magnificent panoramic view, from the Panthéon to the Sacré-Coeur ➡ 112.

Hôtel du Panthéon (54)
19 place du Panthéon, 75005 ☎ 01 43 54 32 95 ➡ 01 43 26 64 65

Ⓜ *Luxembourg* Ⓟ *34 rooms* ●● Ⓥ *F45* 🔲 🔳 📷 🛗 Ⅲ 🍸 🚭 🚭 🌿 ✚ 🌿

This 18th-century building offers a magnificent view of the city, especially room no. 24 which opens onto a terrace. The rooms are light and airy with Louis XVI furniture and Louis-Philippe ceilings with exposed beams.

Hôtel des Grandes Écoles (55)
75 rue du Cardinal-Lemoine, 75005
☎ 01 43 26 79 23 ➡ 01 43 25 28 15

Ⓜ *Cardinal-Lemoine, Monge* Ⓟ *51 rooms* ● Ⓥ *F40* 🔲 📷 🚭 🚭 🚭 ✚

This truly exceptional Paris hotel stands at the end of a cul-de-sac. As you cross the threshold, you enter a miniature paradise of small rooms in a garden setting. Although in the heart of Paris, the peace and quiet of the slightly old-fashioned surroundings create the impression of being deep in the countryside. Breakfast outside to the chirping of the sparrows. As well as its 'rural' setting, this is an eminently affordable hotel which offers warm and friendly service.

Not forgetting
■ **Le Clos Médicis (56)** 56 rue Monsieur-le-Prince, 75006
☎ 01 43 29 10 80 ➡ 01 43 54 26 90 ●●●

Contemporary Provençal-style decor lies behind the 17th-century façade of the Clos Médicis.

In the area

Odéon is the most 'theatrical' of the left-bank districts. If you listen carefully, you may even hear strains of *Le Mariage de Figaro* from the Théâtre de l'Europe ➡ 90. Today, this busy district is the preserve of movie-goers, gourmets and shopaholics.

Where to stay

Prince de Conti (57)
8 rue Guénégaud, 75006 ☎ 01 44 07 30 40 ➡ 01 44 07 36 34

Ⓜ Odéon Ⓟ *26 rooms* ●●● *2 suites F1250* 🍴 *F75* 🔲 Ⓞ *10am–10.30pm* 🔲 📞 🛗 *safe* 🎞 🖥 ✖ ➕

If you are looking for a cozy, English-style hotel, this is the one for you. The 18th-century building, refurbished in 1994, offers excellent facilities. Although its rooms are relatively small, they are always comfortable, and some have balconies that overlook the courtyard.

Relais Christine (58)
3 rue Christine, 75006 ☎ 01 40 51 60 80 ➡ 01 40 51 60 81

Ⓜ Odéon Ⓟ 🏨 *34 rooms* ●●●● *17 suites F2400* 🍴 *F95* 🔲 Ⓞ 🔲 📞 🎞 🛗 🎞 🎬 🌳 💇 ✖ ➕ ➕

Behind a wrought-iron gate, one of the most delightful left-bank hotels occupies a former Augustinian convent and cloister (16th century). The interior decor is warm (rich colors and wood paneling) and in keeping with the traditional style of the building (Liberty prints, beams and roughcast flagstones). There is a charming central courtyard and several very pleasant split-level suites.

Left Bank Saint-Germain Hôtel (59)
9 rue de l'Ancienne-Comédie, 75006
☎ 01 43 54 01 70 ➡ 01 43 26 17 14

Ⓜ Odéon Ⓟ *31 rooms* ●● *1 suite F1400* 🍴 *F50* 🔲 🔲 *satellite* 📞 🛗 🎞 *safe* ✖ 💇

This elegant and comfortable hotel is virtually next door to the Procope and opposite the Ancienne Comédie Française. Furniture in the Louis XVIII style, damask wallpaper, Aubusson tapestry and walnut-paneled alcoves create a romantic atmosphere. The 17th-century building (renovated in 1989) is centered around three gardens and offers a splendid view of Notre-Dame from some of its rooms.

Relais Saint-Germain (60)
9 carrefour de l'Odéon, 75006 ☎ 01 43 29 12 05 ➡ 01 46 33 45 30

Ⓜ Odéon Ⓟ *22 rooms* ●●●● *1 suite F2000* 🍴 *included* 🔲 Ⓞ *6.30am–11pm* 🔲 📞 🛗 🎞 *safe* 🎬 *Le Comptoir du Relais* 🌳 💇 ✖ ➕

Decorated with ancient prints and furniture, this delightful and luxuriously comfortable hotel has named its rooms after famous French authors. The room numbers ending in 4 – e.g. 'Ronsard' (no. 14) and 'Montesquieu' (no. 54) – overlook the street. 'Balzac' (no. 56) is a small, split-level suite with African-style decor. It opens onto a sunny terrace that can, if required, communicate with 'Molière' (no. 58).

Not forgetting

■ **Buci Latin (61)** 34 rue de Buci, 75006 ☎ 01 43 29 07 20 ➡ 01 43 29 67 44 ●●●

■ Where to eat ➡ 76

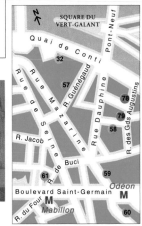

SQUARE DU
VERT-GALANT

Quai de Conti

Pont-Neuf

32

57

Rue de Seine

Rue Mazarine

R. Guénégaud

Rue Dauphine

R. des Gds Augustins

79

79

58

R. Jacob

R. de Buci

61

R. de Buci

59

58

60

61

Boulevard Saint-Germain   **Odéon** M

R. du Four

Mabillon

60

M

61

60

60

The doors of the rooms in the Buci Latin
have all been decorated in different styles
by young artists. One example of the
originality of this delightful little hotel.

60   61   61

Saint-Germain is the literary heart of Paris, with most publishing houses established here. Its legendary cafés are still frequented by intellectuals. It is also becoming a luxury shopping district. ■ Where to eat ➡ 78
■ After dark ➡ 86 ➡ 88 ➡ 98 ■ What to see ➡ 116

Where to stay

Hôtel Montalembert (62)
3 rue Montalembert, 75006 ☎ 01 45 49 68 68 ➡ 01 45 49 69 49

M *Rue du Bac* P 🏠 *51 rooms* ●●●● *5 suites F2830* 📶 *F100* ▭ ⊙ ▣ 🗗
▥ 🛗 ▥ *safe* 🎏 ▮ ⚙ ✂ 🏋 🍴 ✍ ✚ ☼ ▮ *80 04 47 74 62*

This beautiful hotel, situated in the antiques district ➡ 160, is only a stone's throw from the Musée d'Orsay ➡ 116, and the church of Saint-Germain-des-Prés. Fronted by an elegant façade (1926), the Montalembert combines classic style with contemporary detail. Typically Rive Gauche.

Hôtel d'Angleterre (63)
44 rue Jacob, 75006 ☎ 01 42 60 34 72 ➡ 01 42 60 16 93

M *Saint-Germain-des-Prés* P *23 rooms* ●● *4 suites F1400* 📶 *F50* ▭ ▣ 🗗
safe ▮ ✂ 🏋 ✍ ✚

Formerly the British embassy where the treaty of American Independence, signed on September 3, 1783, was prepared. Ernest Hemingway stayed here for some time in room no. 14. Quiet clientele and a historic (predominately Napoleon III-style) decor. Each of the spacious rooms is decorated in a different style and most overlook the central courtyard.

Villa Saint-Germain (64)
29 rue Jacob, 75006 ☎ 01 43 26 60 00 ➡ 01 46 34 63 63

M *Saint-Germain-des-Prés* P *29 rooms* ●●● *3 suites F1600* 📶 *F80* ▭ ⊙
🗗 ▣ ▥ 🛗 *safe* 🏋 ▮ 🎵 *La Villa* ✂ ✍

An ideally situated 19th-century building that has achieved an extremely successful contemporary 'look'. It has the distinctive hallmark of Marie-Christine Dorner, who has used leather, nickel and sanded and marbled glass. It has a very good basement jazz club, La Villa ➡ 98. The hotel is regularly chosen by performers on tour.

Hôtel Guy-Louis Duboucheron (65)
13 rue des Beaux-Arts, 75006 ☎ 01 43 25 27 22 ➡ 01 43 25 64 81

M *Saint-Germain-des-Prés* P *25 rooms* ●●● *2 suites F2800* 📶 *F100* ▭ ⊙
6am–noon ▣ 🗗 ▥ 🛗 ▥ ▮ ⚙ ✂ ✍ ✚

This is one of the most unusual hotels in Paris. Each room has its own story to tell and its own individual decor, often associated with its most famous occupant. For example, framed copies of bills still owing to the hotel hang in the room where Oscar Wilde died (uttering his last words, 'Either this wallpaper goes or I do.'), and the room once occupied by the French actress Mistinguett still contains the furniture she bequeathed to the hotel.

Not forgetting
■ **Hôtel Solférino (66)** 91 rue de Lille, 75007 ☎ 01 47 05 85 54
➡ 01 45 55 51 16 ●● ■ **Lenox (67)** 9 rue de l'Université, 75007
☎ 01 42 96 10 95 ➡ 01 42 61 52 83 ●●

■ Where to
shop ➡ 158

The rooms in the Hôtel Guy-Louis Duboucheron
are centered around a beautifully lit gallery.

63

In striking contrast to the busy left-bank districts of Saint-Germain and Odéon, Sèvres offers a degree of respite and a calmer, more serene lifestyle. An ideal retreat after a day's sightseeing. ■ Where to eat ➡ 78 ➡ 82 ■ After dark ➡ 86 ➡ 88 ■ Where to shop ➡ 140 ➡ 156 ➡ 158

▶ Where to stay

Duc de Saint-Simon (68)
14 rue Saint-Simon, 75007 ☎ 01 44 39 20 20 ➡ 01 45 48 68 25

Ⓜ *Rue-du-Bac* Ⓟ *29 rooms* ●●●● *5 suites F1825* Ⓥ *F70* ▭ Ⓘ *7.30am–10.30pm* ▦ Ⓘ Ⓘ Ⓘ Ⓨ ▨ Ⓚ Ⓧ ▨ ✦

This charming, small 18th-century house, off the rue de Grenelle, with its attractive courtyard, is much in demand from the fashion and art worlds. The rooms are small, but beautifully furnished, and have magnificent bathrooms. Ask for a room overlooking the garden, or rooms 14, 24, 25 or 42, which have terraces.

Hôtel Lutétia (69)
45 boulevard Raspail, 75006 ☎ 01 49 54 46 46 ➡ 01 49 54 46 00

Ⓜ *Sèvres-Babylone* Ⓟ *250 rooms* ●●●● *30 suites F2200* Ⓥ *F85* ▭ Ⓘ ▣ ▦ Ⓘ Ⓘ Ⓘ Ⓨ *Le Lutèce* ▦ *Le Paris* ➡ *78; Brasserie Lutétia* ✦ *Salon Saint-Germain* ▨ Ⓧ ✦ *reception rooms* ▨ ▨

The Hôtel Lutétia is one of the last luxury hotels on the Left Bank. The vast bulk of this huge art deco building reveals nothing of the very distinctive atmosphere of its many rooms and famous bar. Since it was built (1907–10) to accommodate the customers of the Bon Marché department store ➡ 140, famous guests have included General de Gaulle and his wife, who spent their wedding night here. Today, it has become the meeting place par excellence of the worlds of fashion, politics, art and literature. Its rooms have been recently redecorated in elegant 1930s style by Sybille de Margerie. The hotel also has a famous restaurant, Le Paris, and an exclusive bar, Le Lutèce, decorated in red and black by Sonia Rykiel.

Récamier (70)
3bis place Saint-Sulpice, 75006 ☎ 01 43 26 04 89 ➡ 01 46 33 27 73

Ⓜ *Saint-Sulpice* Ⓟ *30 rooms* ● *I suite F900* Ⓥ *F30* ▭ ▦ Ⓚ ▨

A quiet and attractive little hotel in the heart of Saint-Germain-des-Prés, only a minute's walk from the Jardin du Luxembourg ➡ 122. Its rooms have all the basic – if minimalist – comforts and occasionally surprising decor. Choose the rooms overlooking the square and church. Although the least expensive may only have a W.C., they all enjoy a magnificent view. The hotel's delightful entrance, with its graceful canopy, is located in a quiet corner of the place Saint-Sulpice.

Not forgetting

■ **Hôtel des Saints-Pères (71)** 65 rue des Saints-Pères, 75006 ☎ 01 45 44 50 00 ➡ 01 45 44 90 83 ●●●
■ **La Perle (72)** 14 rue des Canettes, 75006 ☎ 01 43 29 10 10 ➡ 01 43 20 10 01 ●●●

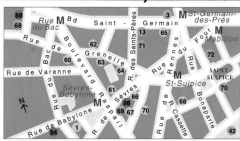

71

69

68

68

Spoilt for choice: romantic style in the Duc de Saint-Simon (room no. 41) or contemporary decor in the Lutétia (Suite Arman).

69

43

Once the haunt of writers and artists, the left-bank district of Montparnasse is now a busy cosmopolitan area boasting a main-line station, movie theaters, shops and myriad restaurants.

■ Where to eat ➥ 48 ➥ 66 ➥ 80 ■ After dark ➥ 86

Where to stay

Hôtel le Saint-Grégoire (73)
43 rue de l'Abbé-Grégoire, 75006 ☎ 01 45 48 23 23 ➥ 01 45 48 33 95

Ⓜ *Saint-Placide* 🅿 *19 rooms* ●● *1 suite F1390* 🎴 *F60* ▬ 🖥 📷 ▥ 📶 *Le Marlotte* 🔟 🍴 ⛷ 🍸

This is more like a house than a hotel. The 18th-century building was decorated by David Hicks who has used kilims as well as his own fabrics, and set off pastel shades with Louis-Philippe sideboards, tables and wardrobes, and paintings tracked down in antique shops. The hotel's clientele (journalists and models) seems to be cast in the same mold and appreciates the charm of this distinctive building.

Hôtel Sainte-Beuve (74)
9 rue Sainte-Beuve, 75006 ☎ 01 45 48 20 07 ➥ 01 45 48 67 52

Ⓜ *Vavin* 🅿 *22 rooms* ●● *1 suite F1550* 🎴 *F80* ▬ 🕐 🖥 📷 📶 ▥ 🔟 🖥 ⛷ 🍸 📺 🍴

Close to the Jardin de Luxembourg ➥ 122, the Musée d'Orsay ➥ 116 and the Musée Rodin ➥ 108, the Sainte-Beuve occupies the perfect location. The David Hicks studio have created restful, English-style interiors in the public rooms, and the spacious private rooms reflect the same feeling of gentility and elegance.

L'Atelier Montparnasse (75)
49 rue Vavin, 75006 ☎ 01 46 33 60 00 ➥ 01 40 51 04 21

Ⓜ *Vavin* 🅿 *17 rooms* ●● *1 suite F950* 🎴 *F40* ▬ 🕐 📷 🖥 📶 🍴 🍸

Not far from the famous La Coupole restaurant ➥ 66, L'Atelier Montparnasse is a small hotel with a very distinctive style. Each room is named after a painter and has a reproduction of a piece of that artist's work reproduced in *pâte-de-verre* mosaic in the bathroom. The reception area hosts temporary exhibitions.

Hôtel Raspail-Montparnasse (76)
203 boulevard Raspail, 75014 ☎ 01 43 20 62 86 ➥ 01 43 20 50 79

Ⓜ *Vavin* 🅿 *38 rooms* ●● *2 suites F1100* 🎴 *F50* ▬ 🖥 📷 📶 ▥ *safe* 🔟 🍴 ⛷ 🍸 📺 ➕ 🍽 📺 *0800 906 454*

In the 19th century, this hotel was known as the Hôtel de la Haute-Loire. The magnificent art nouveau canopy above the entrance – an exact copy of the original canopy that had disappeared – has restored the building to its former glory. The hotel overlooks the Carrefour Vavin and several rooms have a view of the Eiffel Tower. It was refurbished by Serge Pons in elegant art nouveau style, and each bedroom is dedicated to a particular artist and decorated with one of their works.

Not forgetting

■ **Villa des Artistes (77)** 8 rue de la Grande-Chaumière, 75006 ☎ 01 43 26 60 86 ➥ 01 43 54 73 70 ●●

74

76

75

75

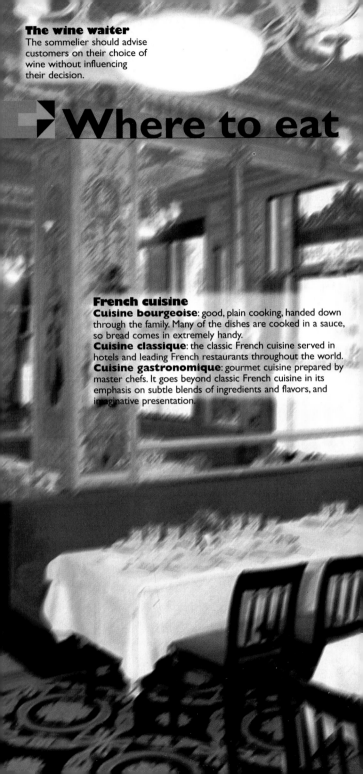

The wine waiter
The sommelier should advise
customers on their choice of
wine without influencing
their decision.

Where to eat

French cuisine
Cuisine bourgeoise: good, plain cooking, handed down
through the family. Many of the dishes are cooked in a sauce,
so bread comes in extremely handy.
Cuisine classique: the classic French cuisine served in
hotels and leading French restaurants throughout the world.
Cuisine gastronomique: gourmet cuisine prepared by
master chefs. It goes beyond classic French cuisine in its
emphasis on subtle blends of ingredients and flavors, and
imaginative presentation.

Prices are inclusive of tax and a 15% service charge, although this doesn't mean you can't leave a tip. The categories below are based on menu prices. But a word of warning, these only apply to lunchtime menus. The 'à la carte' price includes a three-course meal, without wine.

99 Restaurants

THE INSIDER'S FAVORITES

➡ **Where to eat**

Maison Blanche "15 Montaigne" (1)
15 avenue Montaigne, 75008 ☎ 01 47 23 55 99 ➡ 01 47 20 09 56

Ⓜ *Alma-Marceau* 🔆 *Gourmet cuisine* ●●●● ▭ 🍴 ⊙ *Mon.–Fri. noon–2.30pm, 8–10.45pm; Sat. 8–10.45pm; closed in Aug.* 🔆

The decor of this restaurant, built on the roof of the Théâtre des Champs-Élysées ➡ 92, is austere, sophisticated and comfortable. The cuisine, by José Martinez, makes extensive use of seasonal produce and reflects an imaginative culinary flair. Elegant service.

Les Célébrités (2)
61 quai de Grenelle, 75015 ☎ 01 40 58 21 29 ➡ 01 40 58 23 51

Ⓜ *Bir-Hakeim* 🔆 *Gourmet cuisine* ●●● *à la carte F400* ⊙ *daily noon–2.30pm, 7–10pm; closed in Aug.* ▭ 🍷 🔆 🍽 *Le Benkay (same address)*

Master chef Joël Robuchon made his debut here. Today, one of his former sous-chefs, Jacques Sénéchal, continues the tradition of excellence with exquisite dishes such as his prawn and scallop salad.

Morot-Gaudry (3)
8 rue de la Cavalerie, 75015
☎ 01 45 67 06 85 ➡ 01 45 67 55 72

Ⓜ *La Motte-Picquet* Ⓟ *Gourmet cuisine* ●●●● *à la carte F400* ▭ ⊙ *Mon.–Sat. noon–2.30pm, 7.30–10.30pm* 🔆

Jean-Pierre Morot-Gaudry's delightful restaurant offers a truly remarkable view of the Eiffel Tower. An attractive menu offers traditional and modestly innovative cuisine, and an excellent choice of wines from southwestern France. An open-air terrace gives diners a front-row view of the fireworks on July 14!

Not forgetting

■ Ciel de Paris (4)
Tour Montparnasse,
33 avenue du Maine, 75014
☎ 01 40 64 77 64 ●●●
*Great views and classic French
cuisine on the 57th story of the
Montparnasse tower.*

■ Toupary (5)
La Samaritaine,
2 quai du
Louvre, 75001
☎ 01 40 41 29 29
●● *Simple,
affordable food at
this Paris store.*

**■ La Tour
d'Argent (6)**
15–17 quai de la
Tournelle, 75005
☎ 01 43 54 23 31
●●●●●
*Renowned for its duck, its cellar,
exceptional service and its view of
the Seine and Notre-Dame.*

■ À la Courtille (7)
1 rue des Envierges, 75020
☎ 01 46 36 51 59
●● *An underrated view of the
Jardin de Belleville. Great food.*

Basic facts

On Level 2 of the Eiffel Tower ➡ 106, the finest panoramic restaurant in Paris occupies a platform set between the pulleys and wheels that operate the lifts. The magnificent view takes in the Arc de Triomphe, Sacré-Coeur, Grand Palais, Notre-Dame…

➡ **Where to eat**

Jules Verne (8)
Tour Eiffel, South (Level 2), Champs-de-Mars, 75007
☎ **01 45 55 61 44** ➡ **01 47 05 29 41**

Ⓜ *Bir-Hakeim, Champs-de-Mars* ⛰ ***Gourmet cuisine*** ●●●●●
à la carte F700 🁢 🕐 *daily 12.15–2.30pm, 7.30–10.30pm* 🎵 🍽 ☘

The Jules Verne offers an exceptional dining experience – enjoy a magnificent view of Paris at sunset and savor the imaginative and meticulously prepared food of Alain Reix. Bread rolls souffléed with crab and served with creamed prawns or turbot grilled in green-apple juice are just two of the inspired creations of this talented chef; the high price is justified. Piano bar and faultless service. Advance booking essential.

JULES VERNE
RESTAURANT de la TOUR EIFFEL

Trocadéro M Av. du Pdt Wilson
14 10
JARDINS
DU TROCADÉRO
Av. des Nations-Unies
Avenue de New-York
Pont
d'Iéna
Quai   Branly
M
Champ-   TOUR
de-Mars   EIFFEL
              8   8
Av. G. Eiffel
CHAMP-DE-MARS

Some 400 feet above the ground, this restaurant opened in 1983 and was named after the French writer of science fiction and adventure, Jules Verne.

It will come as no surprise that the Place de l'Étoile is a district of prestigious restaurants, the sort that do not bow to short-lived, transitory fashions but remain loyal to established principles. Their relatively high prices are often justified. ■ Where to stay ➡ 18 ➡ 22 ■ After dark

➡ Where to eat

Guy Savoy (9)
18 rue Troyon, 75017 ☎ 01 43 80 40 61 ➡ 01 46 22 43 09

Ⓜ *Charles-de-Gaulle-Étoile* 🍴 **Gourmet cuisine** ●●●●● *à la carte F800* ▢
◯ *Mon.–Fri. 12.30–2.30pm, 7.30–10.30pm; Sat. 7.30–10.30pm* 🎴 *Les Bookinistes* ●● *53 quai des Grands-Augustins, 75006 ☎ 01 43 25 45 94*

Sober but elegant modern decor and inventive cuisine using a limited range of basic flavors in a wide range of subtle variations. Guy Savoy is a chef at the height of his powers, a master of flavor: skate served with caviar and Breton vegetables, mussels and meadow mushrooms. The cellar represents most of the French wine-growing regions, with an especially wide choice of wines from the Rhône. A great restaurant.

Taïra (10)
10 rue des Acacias, 75017 ☎ 01 47 66 74 14

Ⓜ *Argentine* 🅿 **Seafood** ●●● *à la carte F350* ▢ ◯ *Mon.–Fri. noon–2.30pm, 7.30–10pm; Sat. 7.30–10pm*

Taïra Kurihara is a Japanese chef who has trained in the art of French cuisine. His delightful creations, which include 'tataki' salmon and turbot ravioli served with *huîtres de Marennes* (cultivated oysters), are the result of a skilful blend of flavors and herbs and the combined arts of Japanese and French preparation methods. A judicious choice of ingredients.

Élysées du Vernet (11)
25 rue Vernet, 75008 ☎ 01 44 31 98 98 ➡ 01 44 31 85 69

Ⓜ *Charles de Gaulle-Étoile, Georges V* 🍴 **Provençal and gourmet cuisine** ●●●●● ▢ ◯ *Mon.–Fri. noon–2.30pm, 7.30–10pm; closed in Aug. and on public holidays* 🍷

An Edwardian glass roof adorns one of the most elegant hotel restaurants in Paris. Alain Solivérès, a former sous-chef under Alain Ducasse, is renowned for his game served with truffles, and for such specialties as roast Bilbao salt cod, pan-fried duck liver, and ice-cream flavored with roasted cocoa beans.

Taillevent (12)
15 rue Lamennais, 75008 ☎ 01 44 95 15 01 ➡ 01 42 25 95 18

Ⓜ *Georges-V* 🍴 **Gourmet cuisine** ●●●●● ▢ 🍴🍴 ◯ *Mon.–Fri. noon–2.30pm, 7.30–10.30pm; closed May 1, Dec. 25, Jan. 1, July 20–Aug. 20*

For 50 years, Taillevent has been the unrivaled guardian of tradition. Its relatively new dishes – terrine of pigeon and foie gras with leeks – and perennial favorites – lobster 'sausage' (*boudin*) served with white butter sauce – reflect the credo of Jean-Claude Vrinat and his chef, Philippe Legendre. Luxurious decor, sophisticated service and an exceptional cellar.

Not forgetting
■ **Pierre Gagnaire (13)** 6 rue Balzac, 75008 ☎ 01 44 35 18 25 ●●●●●
Simply prepared and beautifully presented cuisine. ■ **Maison Prunier (14)**
16 avenue Victor-Hugo, 75016 ☎ 01 44 17 35 85 ●●●●● *Enjoy the delicate seafood cuisine of Gabriel Biscay in a magnificent art deco setting.*

➡ 86 ➡ 88
➡ 96
■ What to
see ➡ 106

MAISON
PRUNIER

The clean lines of the decor chosen by Guy Savoy and the
newly renovated interior of Taillevent.

The 17th *arrondissement* was originally renowned for its modest restaurants and *cuisine bourgeoise.* Over the last 20 years, the number of top-quality establishments has gradually increased and today the district offers a complete range of places to eat, from gourmet restaurants to

Where to eat

Michel Rostang (15)
20 rue Rennequin, 75017 ☎ 01 47 63 40 77 ➡ 01 47 63 82 75

Ⓜ Ternes 🞤 *Classic French cuisine* ●●●●● *à la carte F600* ▯ 🍴 🕑
Mon.–Fri. noon–2.30pm, 7.30–10.30pm; Sat. 7.30–10.30pm; closed Aug. 1–15
🍴 *Le Bistrot d'à Côté* ➡ 76

Michel Rostang was born and brought up in a region of lakes and Alpine meadows. He often uses freshwater fish and knows how to prepare it to the best advantage. He is one of the few chefs in Paris to offer char lakefish, perch and polar. A cuisine that uses seasonal vegetables (truffles, mushrooms) and traditional produce (Bresse) served in the friendly atmosphere maintained by Marie-Claude Rostang. An excellent choice of wines, ad hoc service.

Pétrissans (16)
30bis avenue Niel, 75017 ☎ 01 42 27 52 03 ➡ 01 40 54 87 56

Ⓜ Ternes Ⓟ *Good, plain cuisine* ●● *à la carte F220* ▯ 🕑 *Mon.–Fri.
noon–2.30pm, 8–10.30pm; closed public holidays, Aug. 1–20* 🍷 🎴

An old wine cellar that has been converted into an atmospheric bistro. Simple cuisine: cheese pâté, house terrines, slow-cooked dishes (braised veal) and other bistro specialties. Friendly, efficient service. Local and vintage wines. Good range of cigars.

Amphyclès (17)
78 avenue des Ternes, 75017 ☎ 01 40 68 01 01 ➡ 01 40 68 91 88

Ⓜ Ternes 🞤 *Gourmet cuisine* ●●●●● *à la carte F600, lunch menu F260* ▯
🕑 *Mon.–Fri. noon–2.30pm, 7–11pm; Sat. 7–11pm*

Philippe Groult, a fiery and creative chef, is a product of the Joël Robuchon school of excellence. His spider crab served in its shell alongside European crab, lobster and crawfish, and his *confit de pigeon* lasagna garnished with truffles achieve the blend of flavors, textures and aromas that is the quintessence of the very greatest French cuisine. Pleasant decor, courteous welcome and service.

Le Petit Colombier (18)
42 rue des Acacias, 75017 ☎ 01 43 80 28 54 ➡ 01 44 40 04 29

Ⓜ Ternes Ⓟ *Classic French cuisine* ●●● *à la carte F350* ▯ 🍴 🕑 *Mon.–Fri.
12.15–2.30pm, 7.15–11.30pm; Sun. 7.15–11.30pm; closed Aug. 1–16*

Old-fashioned decor, a muted atmosphere, a very friendly welcome and the masterly cuisine of Bernard Fournier, based on regional products: tenderloin of beef, lobster from Brittany and French game (when in season). A fine selection of 440 leading wines and a smoking area around an open fireplace.

Not forgetting
■ **Les Béatilles (19)** 11bis rue Villebois-Mareuil, 75017 ☎ 01 45 74 43 80
●●● *Classic French cuisine. Culinary expertise and good-quality ingredients.*
■ **La Marée (20)** 1 rue Daru, 75008 ☎ 01 43 80 20 00 ●●●●● *Seafood.
Originality and tradition in a modestly luxurious setting. Excellent wines.*

modest
bistros.
■ After dark
➡ 100

Michel Rostang continually extends
his menu with dishes from his
native Alps.

The *colline* (hill) of Chaillot, which witnessed the meteoric rise of Joël Robuchon, is today witnessing the success of Alain Ducasse. A district of beautiful tree-lined avenues. ■ Where to eat ➡ 74 ■ Where to stay ➡ 20 ■ What to see ➡ 106

➡ Where to eat

Conti (21)
72 rue Lauriston, 75016 ☎ 01 47 27 74 67 ➡ 01 47 27 37 66

Ⓜ *Boissière* Ⓟ *Italian gourmet cuisine* ●● *à la carte F330* ▭ Ⓒ *Mon.–Fri. noon–2.30pm, 7.15–10.30pm; closed for 3 weeks in Aug., Jan. 1–7*

Michel Ranvier is passionately fond of Italy and takes his interpretation of its culinary repertoire very seriously. People love Italian opera, so why not Italian cuisine? Spaghetti with Mediterranean 'white caviar', scallops in *vin santo* and (in season) white truffles from Alba, are just a few of the specialties of the house. A fine list of Italian wines. Meticulous service. Good range of cigars.

Alain Ducasse (22)
59 avenue Raymond-Poincaré, 75116
☎ 01 47 27 12 27 ➡ 01 47 27 31 22

Ⓜ *Trocadéro* 🔊 *Gourmet cuisine* ●●●●● *à la carte F1200* ▭ ❙❙ Ⓒ *Mon.– Fri. noon–2pm, 7.45–10pm; closed July 4–Aug. 4, Dec. 24–Jan. 4* 🔊 Ⓨ

Alain Ducasse, the first chef of the famous Louis XV restaurant in Monte Carlo, took over from Joël Robuchon on August 12, 1996. Robuchon's perfectionism was succeeded by Ducasse's brilliant contemporary vision of gourmet cuisine: high-precision preparation and an in-depth understanding of ingredients. Eclectic and luxurious decor. A richly stocked cellar lovingly tended by Gérard Margeon.

Jamin (23)
32 rue de Longchamp, 75116 ☎ 01 45 53 00 07 ➡ 01 45 53 00 15

Ⓜ *Trocadéro* Ⓟ *Gourmet cuisine* ●●●● *à la carte F500* ▭ Ⓒ *Mon.–Fri. noon–2.30pm, 7.30–10.15pm; closed July 11–Aug. 4*

The former restaurant of Joël Robuchon (closed since 1993) has been reopened by Benoît Guichard, who has particular style. Pan-fried scallops of foie gras, sweet-and-sour leeks and pig's cheek flavored with marjoram combine perfection and precision in a slightly lower key. Modestly priced wines.

Port Alma (24)
10 avenue de New York, 75116 ☎ 01 47 23 75 11

Ⓜ *Alma-Marceau* *Seafood* ●●● *à la carte F350* ▭ Ⓒ *Mon.–Sat. 12.30– 2.30pm, 7.30–10.30pm; closed in Aug.* 🔊

Paul Canal is a Catalan who is passionate about fresh fish, which he prepares with simplicity and loving care. He seeks to highlight the natural qualities of bass, sole, scallops and abalone by means of simple but effective preparation. Bouillabaisse served on Fridays.

Not forgetting
■ **Faugeron (25)** 52 rue de Longchamp, 75116 ☎ 01 47 04 24 53 ●●●●● *Modesty and dedication are Henri Faugeron's tribute to French cuisine.*

Alain Ducasse's restaurant occupies an early 20th-century mansion and offers an intimate and conventional setting.

Basic facts

The River Seine divides Paris – creating two areas, each with a very different character. Parisians make the most of their river and its banks, not least as attractive places to dine.

➡ Where to eat

Le Don Juan (26)
Yacht de Paris, port de Javel-Haut, 75015
☎ 01 44 37 10 20 ➠ 01 44 37 10 25

Ⓜ *Javel* 🅿 *Gourmet cuisine* ●●●●● ◻ 🕔 *daily: boarding 8.30pm, departure 9pm, return 11pm* 🅐 *Acajou same service*

A superb 1930s yacht that has been luxuriously renovated. Drinks are served on the upper deck, and dinner in the main saloon (26 places) and officers' wardroom (14 places), as you cruise beneath the bridges of Paris to the Grande Bibliothèque. Sophisticated cuisine devised by Gérard Besson, and prepared and served by his crew. A top-of-the-range *bateau mouche* with prices to match.

Pavillon Panama (27)
Port de Javel-Haut, 75015 ☎ 01 44 37 10 21 ➠ 01 44 37 11 25

Ⓜ *Javel* 🅗 *Classic French cuisine* ●● ◻ 🕔 *daily noon–2.30pm, 8–11pm*

A pleasant riverside terrace, situated above the attractive new Parc André Citroën ➠ 123 in this rapidly developing district. The Pavillon has established a sound reputation among people who like something out of the ordinary. Its fish specialties and fashionable dishes (sun-dried tomato tart with warm goat's cheese and vegetable *anchoïade*) attract a trendy clientele. Very popular in fine weather.

La Plage Parisienne (28)
Port de Javel-Haut, 75015 ☎ 01 40 59 41 00 ➠ 01 40 59 81 50

Ⓜ *Javel* 🅗 *Classic French cuisine* ●●● ◻ 🕔 *daily noon–2pm, 8–11.30pm*

In fine weather, what could be more pleasant than to sit beneath the umbrellas of this delightful terrace on the banks of the Seine? Its 'healthy' cuisine of simple salads and vegetable dishes, correctly served, attracts a clientele from the world of fashion and advertising. Definitely out of the ordinary and an ideal place to enjoy a meal with friends, a pleasure enhanced (at lunchtime) by the presence of the sun.

Café Six-huit (29)
Quai Malaquais, 75006/quai Montebello, 75005 ☎ 01 43 80 74 54

Ⓜ *Pont-Neuf* 🅿 *Classic French cuisine* ● 🕔 *Apr.–Sep.: daily noon–3pm, 7–11pm* 🅨 *11pm–2am Café-concert Oct.–Mar.: Mon.–Sat. 7pm–2am*

At the foot of the Passerelle des Arts, you can feast your eyes on the Palais du Louvre, the Pont Neuf and also – between April and September – on what is served on your plate (two affordable lunch and dinner menus). For the rest of the year, the boat is a floating *café-concert* moored at the Quai Montebello. Relaxed, friendly atmosphere.

Not forgetting

■ **Bermuda Onion (30)** 16 rue Linois, 75015 ☎ 01 45 75 11 11 ●●●
Flavorsome classic French cuisine and mixed clientele at this showcase restaurant where people come to see and be seen. Large terrace overlooking the Seine. Background music. Ideal for Sunday brunch.

28

26

29

28

26

26

In the area

In the 19th century, the Champs-Élysées replaced the Palais Royal and the grands boulevards as the fashionable place to be seen. Today, the recently renovated avenue is preparing for the new millennium. Its gardens and the neighboring avenues offer an ideal opportunity for an

Where to eat

L'Astor (31)
11 rue d'Astorg, 75008 ☎ 01 53 05 05 20 ➡ 01 53 05 05 30

🅜 *Saint-Augustin* 🏵 *Gourmet cuisine* ●●● *à la carte F350* 🔲 🍴 🕒 *Mon.–Fri. noon–2pm, 7.30–10pm* 🆈

Although Joël Robuchon is not actively involved in its preparation, he keeps a close eye on the cuisine of the Hôtel Astor ➡ 26. Those who have never tasted – or who cannot live without – caviar in aspic served with creamed cauliflower, prawn ravioli garnished with truffles and served with cabbage or the famous potato purée, should make their pilgrimage to this elegant restaurant with its glass roof, cabled columns and efficient service.

Ailleurs (32)
26 rue Jean-Mermoz, 75008 ☎ 01 53 53 98 00 ➡ 01 53 53 98 01

🅜 *Franklin-Roosevelt* 🅿 *International* ● *lunch menu F90* 🔲 🕒 *Mon.–Fri. noon–3pm, 8–11.30pm; Sat. 8–11.30pm* 🆈

This richly decorated restaurant with bar serves dishes from around the globe. Side-by-side on the menu are such specialties as Andalusian gaspacho, chicken tagine, sashimi, tempura and Provence vegetables. The clientele, members of the fashion set and business diners, reflects the area.

Laurent (33)
41 avenue Gabriel, 75008 ☎ 01 42 25 00 39 ➡ 01 45 62 45 21

🅜 *Champs-Élysées-Clemenceau* 🏵 *Gourmet cuisine* ●●●● *à la carte F700* 🔲 🍴 🕒 *Mon.–Fri. 12.30–2.30pm, 7.30–11pm; Sat 7.30–11pm; closed public holidays* 🎫

This exceptional restaurant in its garden setting is a monument to the Paris restaurant trade. Judging by the hare and mushroom ravioli and the smoked bass served with soured buttery green cabbage, it is also a high-flying restaurant. It is managed by Philippe Braun, and Philippe Bourgignon keeps a very fine cellar.

Ledoyen (34)
1 avenue Dutuit, Carré des Champs-Élysées, 75008
☎ 01 53 05 10 01 ➡ 01 47 42 55 01

🅜 *Franklin-Roosevelt* 🏵 *Gourmet cuisine* ●●● *à la carte F800* 🔲 🍴 🕒 *Mon.–Fri. noon–2pm, 7.30–10.30pm; closed in Aug.* 🆈 ⓘ *Cercle Ledoyen (same address)* **Classic French cuisine** ●●●● ☎ 01 53 05 10 02

Ghislaine Arabian is still delighting Parisians with a very personal brand of cuisine, inspired by the flavors of her native Flanders. Indulge your taste buds with minute-smoked-mussel soup with churned buttermilk or turbot cooked in beer with fried onions. Wonderful French fries.

Not forgetting

⬛ **Lasserre (35)** 17 avenue Franklin D. Roosevelt, 75008
☎ 01 43 59 53 43 ●●●●● *A historic restaurant with a celebrity clientele. Duck à l'orange a specialty.*

after-dinner stroll. ■ Where to stay ➡ 22 ➡ 26 ■ What to see ➡ 108 ■ Where to shop ➡ 142

35

34

In 1791, Antoine Nicolas Doyen rented a café on the Champs-Élysées and converted it into a restaurant.

8ᵉ Arrᵗ

AVENUE
DES
CHAMPS ÉLYSÉES

34

35

33

Where to eat

Lucas Carton (36)
9 place de la Madeleine, 75008 ☎ 01 42 65 22 90 ➡ 01 42 65 06 23

Ⓜ *Madeleine* 🎩 **Gourmet cuisine** ●●●● *à la carte F1000* ⊟ ▮▮ ⏰ *Mon.– Fri. noon–2.30pm, 8–10.30pm; Sat. 8–10.30pm; Aug. 1–21* 🈂

Alain Senderens has become the guardian of this temple to innovative, as opposed to opportunist, cuisine. He is an impassioned perfectionist, achieving a precise balance of flavors and aromas and complementing his dishes with carefully chosen wines. Although his duck *Apicius* and hare *à la Royale* (simmered in red wine) are perennial masterpieces, each season brings a range of new dishes. A truly exceptional restaurant.

Les Ambassadeurs (37)
10 place de la Concorde, 75008 ☎ 01 44 71 16 16 ➡ 01 44 71 15 02

Ⓜ *Concorde* 🎩 **Gourmet cuisine** ●●●● *à la carte F600* ⊟ ▮▮ ⏰ *daily noon–2.30pm, 7–10.30pm* ▯ 🈂

Les Ambassadeurs forms part of Le Crillon ➡ 24, and is famed as one of the city's most beautiful luxury-hotel restaurants. Its elegant and amiable service also make it one of the most convivial. Frédéric Le Sel reinterprets classic dishes without flouting established principles. Marble and gilt decor.

Le Carré des Feuillants (38)
14 rue de Castiglione, 75001 ☎ 01 42 86 82 82 ➡ 01 42 86 07 71

Ⓜ *Concorde* 🅿 **Gourmet cuisine** ●●●●● *à la carte F550* ⊟ ⏰ *Mon.–Fri. noon–2.30pm, 7.30–10.30pm; Sat. 7.30–10.30pm; closed in Aug*

Alain Dutournier's cuisine may be inspired by the mountain streams of the Pyrenees and the River Adour, but it is far from being a mere repetition of the obvious regional dishes. A light touch, precise cooking and a carefully calculated use of chili peppers from the Basque village of Espelette give his roasted prawns a truly exquisite flavor. Fine cellar and meticulous service.

À la Grille Saint-Honoré (39)
**15 place du Marché Saint-Honoré, 75001
☎ 01 42 61 00 93 ➡ 01 47 03 31 64**

Ⓜ *Concorde* 🅿 **Good, plain cuisine** ●● *à la carte F230* ⊟ ⏰ *Tue.–Sat. noon–2.30pm, 7–10.30pm; closed Aug. 1–20*

Generously cooked traditional ingredients, served in the old-fashioned comfort of a bistro whose chef is keen to improve on classic recipes: game when it is in season, shellfish when they are affordable and frogs' legs. A study in professionalism and tranquility.

Not forgetting
■ **Goumard-Prunier (40)** 9 rue Duphot, 75001 ☎ 01 42 60 36 07 ●●●●● *An elaborate art deco setting and elegantly sophisticated seafood.*
■ **Le Meurice (41)** Hôtel Meurice ➡ 24 ☎ 01 44 58 10 10 ●●●● *Louis XVI decor, gourmet cuisine by Marc Marchand. Excellent cellar.*

■ Where to
shop ➡ 146
➡ 148 ➡ 150

31 Madeleine **M**

MADELEINE

R. D. Casanova
R. Gomboust
Place
du Marché
St-Honoré
PLACE
VENDÔME

Rue Boissy-d'Anglas
Rue Royale
Rue St-Florentin
Rue Saint-Honoré
Rue du Mont-Thabor
Rue de Castiglione
Rue de Rivoli

Concorde **M** Tuileries
PLACE DE LA
CONCORDE
JARDIN DES
TUILERIES

41

36

40

LUCAS·CARTON
Alain Senderens

36

Gourmand Praniers

40

Almost 200 years separate
Robert Lucas and Francis
Carton, who gave their
names to one of the finest
restaurants in Paris.

38

41

The memory of the Second Empire is kept alive in several restaurants in the Opéra district, which played a major role in the life of Paris during the golden age of the *grand boulevard*. A number of brasseries and bistros maintain the culinary tradition. ■ Where to stay ➡ 28 ■ After dark

➡ Where to eat

L'Œnothèque (42)
20 rue Saint-Lazare, 75009 ☎ 01 48 78 08 76 ➡ 01 40 16 10 27

Ⓜ *Notre-Dame-de-Lorette* **Good, plain cuisine** ●●● ▣ Ⓢ *Mon.–Fri. noon–2.30pm, 7.30–11pm; closed Aug. 7–31* ▦

This local restaurant occupies a former liquor store and has unusual decor: wall-to-wall bottles. The proprietor, Daniel Hallée, was a *sommelier* at Jamin ➡ 56 and the chef, Hallée's son William, trained with Alain Dutournier. The cuisine – saddle of hare (in season), magnificent fish dishes and excellent beef – is complemented by excellent regional wines and Havana cigars.

Casa Olympe (43)
48 rue Saint-Georges, 75009 ☎ 01 42 85 26 01 ➡ 01 45 26 49 33

Ⓜ *Notre-Dame-de-Lorette* 🔊 **Classic French cuisine** ●● ▣ Ⓢ *Mon.–Fri. noon–2pm, 8–11pm; closed Aug., Dec. 24–Jan. 2*

Once the culinary queen of Montparnasse, Olympe, aka Dominique Versini, is returning to her roots with this modest bistro. The richly flavored dishes include roasted guinea fowl, casserole of free-range pork and sage, and Sisteron lamb. Brisk service. Moderate prices.

Saint-Amour (44)
8 rue Port-Mahon, 75002 ☎ 01 47 42 63 82

Ⓜ *Opéra* Ⓟ **Classic French cuisine** ●● *à la carte F250* ▣ Ⓢ *Mon.–Fri. noon–2.30pm, 7–10.15pm; Sat. 7–10.15pm; closed pubic holidays, Sat., Sun. during July and Aug.*

This modest two-story restaurant, which witnessed Édith Piaf's debut in Paris, reflects a discerning taste for the good things in life. It offers classic French dishes from Lyons and Burgundy washed down with a simple Beaujolais or another of its wide range of very reasonably priced wines. *Turbot au sel de Guérande* (salt turbot) and chocolate tart are two of the house favorites.

Drouant (45)
16–18 rue Gaillon, 75002 ☎ 01 42 65 15 16 ➡ 01 49 24 02 15

Ⓜ *Opéra* 🔊 ▣ Ⓢ **Gourmet cuisine** ●●●●● *à la carte F500* 🍴 *daily noon–2.30pm, 7–10.30pm* **Café Drouant** ●● *daily noon–2.30pm, 7pm–midnight* ▮

This traditional restaurant is famous for its wrought-iron staircase by the interior designer, Jacques-Émile Ruhlmann, its 'marine' ceiling decorated with fish, shellfish and crustaceans, and its Salon Goncourt. Louis Grondard's cuisine deserves equal attention for its precise cooking, presentation and classic authenticity. Magnificent rooms on the upper floor where Jean Cocteau and Colette were regulars. Excellent wine list and impeccable service.

Not forgetting

■ **La Villa Créole (46)** 19 rue d'Antin, 75002 ☎ 01 47 42 64 92 ●●● *Flavorsome Caribbean cuisine featuring fish and spices.*

➥ 88 ➥ 90 ➥
92 ■ Where
to shop ➥ 140
➥ 150

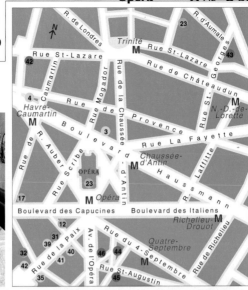

43

45

42

45

44

45

Some Parisian restaurants have become symbols of the city, recognized around the world. Many conjure up a particular era in the city's history, and boast wonderfully evocative interiors. Some have been connected with the literati of the city, and resonate with memories of a bygone era.

Where to eat

Le Pré Catelan (47)
Route de Suresnes, 75016 ☎ 01 44 14 41 14 ➡ 01 45 24 43 25

(Bois de Boulogne) **M** *Porte Dauphine* 🍽 **Gourmet cuisine** ●●●●● *à la carte F550* 🖃 ▮▮ ⏱ *Tue.–Sat. noon–2.30pm, 7–10.30pm; Sun. noon–2.30pm; closed for a fortnight in Feb.* ▮ ✴

Roland Durand maintains the gourmet tradition of this *fin-de-siècle* monument in the Bois de Boulogne. His technically brilliant, distinctively flavored and positively exquisite cuisine is original and varied: caramelized pigs' trotters served with truffles, or duck roasted with tamarind. Excellent cellar and meticulous service.

Maxim's (48)
3 rue Royale, 75008
☎ 01 42 65 27 94 ➡ 01 40 17 02 91

M *Concorde* 🍽 **Classic French cuisine** ●●●●● 🖃 ▮▮ ⏱ *Mon.–Sat. 12.30pm–2pm, 7.30–10.15pm; closed Sun.–Mon. during July and Aug.* 🎵 🚫

Wonderful art nouveau decor (1893). A place to be seen and to see, but until recently no longer at the cutting edge of great cuisine. However, Michel Kérever, chef here since 1996, aims to change that.

Chartier (49)
7 rue du Faubourg-Montmartre, 75009
☎ 01 47 70 86 29 ➡ 01 48 24 14 68

M *Montmartre* **P** **Home cooking** ● *à la carte F100* 🖃 ⏱ *daily 11.30am–3pm., 6–10pm* 🚫

A vestige of late-19th-century, working-class Paris when 'home cooking' was served in a luxurious setting, Chartier has lost none of its popularity and still serves good, plain dishes. An interesting and unusual place to eat.

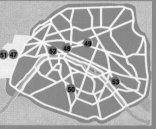

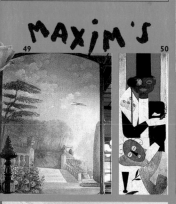

MAXIM'S

La Coupole (50)
102 boulevard du
Montparnasse, 75014
☎ 01 43 20 14 20
→ 01 43 35 46 14

M *Vavin, Montparnasse* P *Classic French cuisine* ●● *à la carte F180* ▤ ◉ *daily 7.30pm–2am; closed Dec. 24* ▥ ♫

A 1920s Paris institution with huge dining room and wonderful decor. Controversially restored in 1988. Best for Sunday lunch or dinner.

Not forgetting

■ **La Grande Cascade (51)** Allée de Longchamp, bois de Boulogne, 75016 ☎ 01 45 27 33 51 ●●●●● One of the 'meccas' of Parisian cuisine since the Second Empire, now under the watchful eye of Alain Ducasse. ■ **La Fermette Marbœuf (52)** 5 rue Marbœuf, 75008 ☎ 01 53 23 08 00 ●● Magnificent art deco settings, classic French cuisine. ■ **Le Train Bleu (53)** Gare de Lyon, place Louis-Armand, 75012 ☎ 01 43 43 09 06 ●●● Superb Edwardian railway architecture. Unfortunately, meals are not always on time.

Montmartre is busy with tourists throughout the year, and many of its restaurants are overpopulated and overpriced. However, if you avoid the main streets you can find some traditional gems. ■ After dark ➡ 92 ■ What to see ➡ 112

 # Where to eat

Le Restaurant (54)
32 rue Véron, 75018 ☎ 01 42 23 06 22

Ⓜ Abbesses Ⓟ *Good, plain cuisine* ● *à la carte F120* ☐ Ⓥ *Mon., Sat. 8–11.30pm; Tue.–Fri. noon–2.30pm, 7.30–11.30pm*

Enjoy a pleasant interlude in this restaurant whose chef is a native of Pau and, not surprisingly, a devotee of gourmet cuisine. It is situated in the rue des Abbesses, an area of Montmartre that is late to bed and late to rise. A beautifully bright, peaceful restaurant in which to enjoy good, plain cuisine. Affordable prices.

A. Beauvilliers (55)
52 rue Lamarck, 75018 ☎ 01 42 54 54 42 ➠ 01 42 62 70 30

Ⓜ Lamarck-Caulaincourt 🔝 *Gourmet cuisine* ●●● *à la carte F500* ☐ Ⓥ *Mon. 7.30–10.45pm; Tue.–Sat. noon–2pm, 7.30–10.45pm* 🚫 🚭

Everything in Édouard Carlier's restaurant contributes to the dining experience, from the delightful decor and slightly old-fashioned menu, to the efficient service and the delicious dishes from the past. A meal here is a true celebration, but one that can prove costly. Keep an eye on the *sommelier!*

Table d'Anvers (56)
2 place d'Anvers, 75009 ☎ 01 48 78 35 21 ➠ 01 45 26 66 65

Ⓜ Anvers Ⓟ *Modern gourmet cuisine* ●●● *à la carte F400* ☐ Ⓥ *Mon.–Fri. noon–2.30pm, 7–10pm; Sat. 7–11pm*

Innovative brothers Christian and Philippe Conticini combine forces in this welcoming restaurant. Christian concentrates on the savory dishes, experimenting with taste, texture and flavor, while Philippe focuses on wonderful desserts. Eclectic wine list.

L'Alsaco (57)
10 rue Condorcet, 75009 ☎ 01 45 26 44 31

Ⓜ Anvers Ⓟ *Alsatian cuisine* ● *à la carte F120* ☐ Ⓥ *Mon.–Fri. 9am–3.30pm, 7–11pm; Sat 7–11pm; closed in Aug.*

Typically simple cuisine and beer and a range of Alsatian wines at reasonable prices. Claude Steger, known as Klaus, has his cold meats sent from the Upper Rhine, and his magnificent sauerkraut from Masevaux. Often full, although the *patron's* mood is as variable as the tab.

Not forgetting

■ **Le Moulin à Vins (58)** 6 rue Burq, 75018 ☎ 01 42 52 81 27 ●●
Open until 2am. The main attractions are Dany, the 'patronne' and her Côtes du Rhône.
■ **Aux Négociants (59)** 27 rue Lambert, 75018 ☎ 01 46 06 15 11 ●●
Wines from the Loire to accompany the rillons (pork belly pieces cooked in lard until crisp), boudin (black pudding) and other specialties from the Loire valley.

55

Dinner at Beauvilliers is an experience to remember.

56

In the area

Before the French Revolution, Paris had a mere 50 restaurants. The first establishment to offer *à la carte* was founded in 1782 in the rue de Richelieu. ■ Where to stay ➡ 30 ➡ 32 ■ After dark ➡ 90 ➡ 98 ➡ 102 ■ What to see ➡ 110 ■ Where to shop ➡ 152 ➡ 154 ➡ 160

Where to eat

Le Grand Véfour (60)

17 rue de Beaujolais, 75001 ☎ 01 42 96 56 27 ➡ 01 42 86 80 71

M *Palais-Royal* 🎩 **Gourmet cuisine** ●●●●● *à la carte F600* ◻ 🍴
🕐 *Mon.–Fri. 12.30–2.15pm, 7.30–10.15pm; closed in Aug.* 🚭

Le Grand Véfour, beneath the arcades of the Palais-Royal, is one of the oldest and most famous of Paris restaurants. Today it is managed by Guy Martin, a native of Savoy, who maintains the restaurant's exceptionally high standard of cuisine. Le Véfour offers its well-to-do clientele a choice of simply prepared dishes, or creations based on what Escoffier called 'the great transformation'. Remarkable cellar and service.

Gérard Besson (61)

5 rue du Coq-Héron, 75001 ☎ 01 42 33 14 74 ➡ 01 42 33 85 71

M *Louvre-Rivoli, Palais-Royal* P **Gourmet cuisine** ●●●●● *à la carte F500* ◻
🕐 *Mon.–Fri. noon–2.30pm, 7.15–10.30pm; Sat. 7.15–10.30pm*

The extensive culinary repertoire of Gérard Besson, a former student of Garin, is based on truffles and game. Scrambled eggs with truffles and noisettes of venison, complemented by a bottle of Burgundy, are among the culinary delights to be enjoyed in the modern decor of this former store in Les Halles. The chef insists on a respectful use of seasonal ingredients, and produces some wonderful new dishes.

Café Marly (62)

Palais du Louvre, 93 rue de Rivoli, 75001 ☎ 01 49 26 06 60

M *Louvre-Rivoli, Palais-Royal* P **Classic French cuisine** ●● 🕐 *daily 8–2am* ◻

One of the trendiest cafés in Paris, Café Marly is located inside the Louvre. Vast rooms with bay windows overlooking the glass pyramid, and a view over the museum rooms devoted to French sculpture. Go in the evening when the pyramid is lit up.

Ambassade d'Auvergne (63)

**22 rue du Grenier-Saint-Lazare, 75003
☎ 01 42 72 31 22 ➡ 01 42 78 85 47**

M *Rambuteau* P **Regional cuisine from the Auvergne and Aveyron** ●● *à la carte F200* ◻ 🕐 *daily noon–2pm, 7.30–10.30pm*

In spite of its rather eccentric and medieval appearance, the restaurant is popular with lovers of *tripoux* (highly seasoned variety meats tied up in small packs with gut casings) and other specialties from the Auvergne region. Regional wines.

Not forgetting

■ **Le Pied de Cochon (64)** 6 rue Coquillière, 75001 ☎ 01 40 13 77 00 ●● *According to a sign over the bar, 'All roads lead to Le Pied de Cochon'. Open round the clock.*
■ **Auberge Nicolas Flamel (65)** 51 rue de Montmorency, 75003 ☎ 01 42 71 77 78 ● *Simple cuisine served in the former house (1407) of the alchemist Nicolas Flamel.*

"If I hadn't got Louis [Vaubale] to take over the 'Véfour', the Americans would have bought the decor and taken it away''. *Jean Cocteau*

In the area

The Marais, one of the most historic districts of Paris, is today a lively area and the center of the city's gay scene. ■ Where to stay ➡ 32 ■ After dark ➡ 92 ■ What to see ➡ 110 ■ Where to shop ➡ 160

Where to eat

Miraville (66)
72 quai de l'Hôtel-de-Ville, 75004
☎ 01 42 74 72 22 ➡ 01 42 74 67 55

Ⓜ *Hôtel-de-Ville, Pont-Marie* Ⓟ **Gourmet cuisine** ●●● *à la carte F350* 🔲 🕒 *Mon.–Fri. noon–2.15pm, 7.30–10.30pm; Sat. 7.30–10.30pm; closed for 3 weeks in Aug.* 🔥 🔆

Alain Lamaison's menu has its roots in southwestern France, between the Landes and the Pays Basque. Sea bream with *chorizo* sausage and *piperade* sauce is characteristic of this aromatic and spicy cuisine with its distinctive flavors. A few very popular dishes – such as the head-of-veal terrine with sun-dried tomatoes – are served throughout the year.

Le Monde des Chimères (67)
69 rue Saint-Louis-en-l'Île, 75004
☎ 01 43 54 45 27 ➡ 01 43 29 84 88

Ⓜ *Pont-Marie* Ⓟ **Good, plain cuisine** ● *à la carte F240* 🔲 🕒 *Tue.–Sat. 12.15–2.30pm, 7.15–10.30pm*

Le Monde des Chimères became famous during the golden age of Nouvelle Cuisine. Today, Cécile Ibane uses her expertise to teach the younger generation that cuisine – like life – goes on. Splendid, slow-cooked dishes of Mediterranean inspiration.

L'Ambroisie (68)
9 place des Vosges, 75004 ☎ 01 42 78 51 45

Ⓜ *Saint-Paul* 🔆 **Gourmet cuisine** ●●●●● 🔲 🍴 🕒 *Tue.–Sat. noon–1.45pm, 8–9.45pm; closed for a fortnight in Feb., 3 weeks in Aug.* 🔆

Bernard Pacard's style is based on the simple presentation of complex flavors using the very best ingredients. His cuisine – precise and faultless – encapsulates the best of gourmet cuisine, and on the place des Vosges to boot! The charlotte of foie gras from the Landes flavored with fennel and spiced caramel is an absolute must. Efficient, friendly service under the watchful eye of M. Pierre, a connoisseur of vintage wines and spirits.

Bofinger (69)
5–7 rue de la Bastille, 75004 ☎ 01 42 72 87 82 ➡ 01 42 72 97 68

Ⓜ *Bastille* Ⓟ **Alsatian cuisine** ●● *à la carte F200* 🔲 🕒 *Mon.–Fri. noon–3pm, 6.30pm–1am; Sat.–Sun. noon–1am*

Bofinger's clientele continues to enjoy the famous sauerkraut, seafood and essentially simple and soberly prepared cuisine beneath the restaurant's magnificent glass roof. Although the regulars of 30 years' standing had some reservations about the change of ownership, by and large the restaurant has remained as popular as in its heyday.

Not forgetting

■ **La Baracane (70)** 38 rue des Tournelles, 75004 ☎ 01 42 71 43 33 ●● *The 'confit de canard' washed down with a bottle of Cahors is said to guarantee long life. In any event, it's just what the doctor ordered!*

The decor (1919) of the Bofinger, by the architect Legay and the interior designer Mitdgen, is considered to be the archetypal brasserie.

Basic facts
Paris has many international restaurants where customers can enjoy
dishes created from fresh ingredients flown in from all over the world.
The city has several thousand Asian restaurants; Chinese cuisine is
particularly popular, as is the more aromatic and lighter Vietnamese

➡ Where to eat

Kim Anh (71)
15 rue de l'Église, 75015 ☎ 01 45 79 40 96 ➠ 01 40 59 49 78

Ⓜ *Charles-Michel* Ⓟ **Gourmet Vietnamese cuisine** 🔲 ●●● *à la carte F250*
▣ 🕐 *daily 7.30–11.30pm*

75

Vietnamese cuisine and tradition bring the
delights of southeast Asia to Paris. Kim Anh,
which offers a delightful family welcome and
an intimate atmosphere, is popular with
celebrities, business people and gourmets.
Spring rolls, stuffed crab, prawns marinated in
curry sauce, steamed stuffed snails, filleted
cockerel and Tonkinese soup. Wines include
Côtes du Jura, Saint-Julien and Graves.

Bertie's (72)
**Hôtel Baltimore, 1 rue Léo-Delibes, 75016
☎ 01 44 34 54 34 ➠ 01 44 34 54 44**

Ⓜ *Boissières* 🎩 **English cuisine** ●●● *à la carte*
F300 ▣ 🕐 *daily 12.30–2pm, 7.30–10.30pm;
closed Aug. 1–15* Ⓨ

Located in the discreetly comfortable Hôtel
Baltimore, this restaurant is named after
Queen Victoria's husband, Prince Albert,
known affectionately as 'Bertie'. Blond oak
decor, large plaid-covered bench seats and
pictures of the British royal family. Specialties:
carved meats served from the trolley, roast
Scottish lamb with mint sauce, roast duck
with orange sauce, sherry trifle. Service
quintessentially British.

76

Mansouria (73)
**11 rue Faidherbe, 75011
☎ 01 43 71 00 16 ➠ 01 40 24 21 97**

Ⓜ *Faidherbe-Chaligny* **Moroccon cuisine** ●●● *à
la carte F200* ▣ 🕐 *Mon. 7.30–11.30pm;
Tue.–Sat. noon–2.30pm, 7.30–11.30pm*

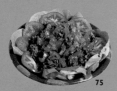
75

The famous Moroccan couscous offers a rich
intensity of flavors: delicious meats accompany
the grain, sauce and vegetables. The hostess,
Fatima Hal, is also a sociologist and has
written a book on this exceptional 'communal
cuisine'. The house specialty is couscous made
with lamb and conserve of onions.

73

74

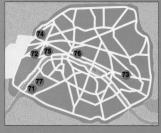

cuisine. North African and European – especially Italian – culinary traditions are also well represented.

73

Tagine, couscous, mint tea, grissini sushi, taboulé, khobz… Unusual and evocative names that conjure up images of exotic lands and flavors.

73

74

75

77

Not forgetting

■ **Paolo Petrini (74)** 6 rue du Débarcadère, 75017 ☎ 01 45 74 25 95
●●●● *Paolo Petrini has introduced Parisians to sophisticated Italian cuisine, inspired by his native Tuscany and characterized by subtle flavors and the very best ingredients. Even if the welcome is sometimes rather reserved, the restaurant is currently one of the best in Paris.*

■ **Pavillon Noura (75)** 21 avenue Marceau, 75116 ☎ 01 47 20 33 33
●●●● *This Lebanese restaurant offers a varied and constantly changing menu.*

■ **Kinugawa (76)** 9 rue du Mont-Thabor, 75001 ☎ 01 42 60 65 07
●●●●● *One of the best Japanese restaurants in Paris where flavor takes precedence over ceremony. Minimalist decor, high prices.*

■ **Chen Soleil d'Est (77)** 15 rue Théâtre, 75015 ☎ 01 45 79 34 34
●●●● *The best Chinese restaurant in Paris, situated in the Chinese quarter. Exceptional Peking duck.*

72

71

In the area

After World War II, Saint-Germain-des-Prés became the center of the city's intellectual life and nightlife. In the 1980s the spotlight was turned on fashion, but the district retains its fine restaurants. ■ Where to stay ➡ 34 ➡ 38 ■ After dark ➡ 90 ➡ 96 ■ What to see ➡ 118 ➡ 120

Where to eat

Le Relais Louis XIII (78)
8 rue des Grands-Augustins, 75006 ☎ 01 43 26 75 96

Ⓜ Saint-Michel ▦ *Classic French cuisine* ●●● *à la carte* F350 ▱ ◷ *Mon. 7.30–10.15pm; Tue.–Sat. noon–2.30pm, 7.30–10.15pm; closed for 1 week in Feb., Aug. 1–21*

The truly amazing medieval and Renaissance decor was designed by an art connoisseur who is also a flea-market enthusiast. The restaurant has been taken over by Manuel Martinez, former chef of La Tour d'Argent ➡ 48. One of a number of restaurants in the area serving diverse and unusual dishes. Good wine list.

Jacques Cagna (79)
14 rue des Grands-Augustins, 75006
☎ 01 43 26 49 39 ➡ 01 43 54 54 48

Ⓜ Saint-Michel ▦ *Gourmet cuisine* ●●●●● *à la carte* F600 ▱ 🍽 ◷ *Mon.– Fri. noon–2pm, 7.30–10.30pm; Sat. 7.30–10.30pm; closed Aug. 1–22, Dec 24–Jan 2*

The restaurant's classic cuisine is in keeping with the 'old Paris' setting in the style of an old inn. Updated classics include leg of pheasant served with cabbage or whole filleted young partridge. First-class cuisine always on the lookout for new ideas. Attentive service.

La Timonerie (80)
35 quai de la Tournelle, 75005 ☎ 01 43 25 44 42

Ⓜ Maubert-Mutualité ℗ *Gourmet cuisine* ●●● ▱ ◷ *Mon. 7.30–10.30pm; Tue.–Sat. noon–2.30pm, 7.30–10.30pm; closed in Aug.*

A quayside restaurant that offers convivial and minimalist decor in the form of a rustic cabin with bare wood walls. In time, the chef's ability to create such deliciously voluptuous and innovative cuisine should take him into the luxury restaurant category. He can often be seen in the restaurant expounding his culinary credo.

Le Bistrot d'à Côté (81)
16 boulevard Saint-Germain, 75005
☎ 01 43 54 59 10 ➡ 01 43 29 02 08

Ⓜ Maubert-Mutualité ℗ *Regional cuisine* ●● ▱ ◷ *Mon.–Fri. noon–2.30pm, 7.30–11pm; Sat. 7.30–11pm* 🍽 Michel Rostang ➡ 54

Le Bistrot offers top-quality, inexpensive cuisine in a classic 1950s setting that was formerly the illustrious *Raffatin et Honorine*. Game is a specialty. Wine served by the glass.

Not forgetting

■ **Allard (82)** 41 rue Saint-André-des-Arts, 75006 ☎ 01 43 26 48 23 ●●● *The new proprietors have successfully maintained the bistro cuisine of Fernande Allard.*

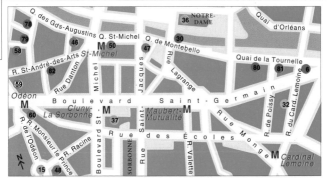

79

79

81

The 17th-century façade of Jacques Cagna, in a quiet street that runs down to the banks of the River Seine.

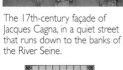

82

80

82

In the area

This district's many eating places, which include some famous restaurants, attract workers from the government ministries and many publishing houses located here. ■ Where to eat ➡ 82 ■ Where to stay ➡ 40 ➡ 42 ■ After dark ➡ 94 ■ What to see ➡ 108 ➡ 116

Where to eat

Le Divellec (83)
107 rue de l'Université, 75007 ☎ 01 45 51 91 96 ➡ 01 45 51 31 75

Ⓜ *Invalides* �%🔼 *Seafood* ●●●●● *à la carte* F600 ▨ 🔌 Ⓢ *Tue.–Sat.* 12.30–2.30pm, 8–10pm; closed Dec. 24, Jan. 1 🈴 🔆

This veritable *conservatoire* of marine delicacies, where the catch is always fresh whatever the cost, attracts a clientele of celebrities and devotees of Jacques Le Divellec's famous seafood cuisine. His talent and force of circumstance have made Le Divellec a historic restaurant in its time, a 20th-century equivalent of the famous Rocher de Cancale.

L'Arpège (84)
84 rue de Varenne, 75007 ☎ 01 45 51 47 33 ➡ 01 44 18 98 39

Ⓜ *Varenne* Ⓟ *Modern gourmet cuisine* ●●●●● *à la carte* F800 ▨ 🔌 Ⓢ *Mon.–Fri.* 12.30–2pm, 7.30–10.30pm; Sun. 7.30–10.30pm

The asceticism of the surroundings here serves only to highlight the brilliance of the dishes prepared by Michel Passard. The genius of this chef lies in his culinary method, precise cooking and preparation techniques. Dedicated service in this top Paris restaurant – located in a quiet district not far from the Musée Rodin ➡ 108 – where cuisine is an art form.

Le Rouge Vif (85)
48 rue de Verneuil, 75007 ☎ 01 42 86 81 87

Ⓜ *Rue-du-Bac* Ⓟ *Good, plain cooking* ● *à la carte* F140 ▨ Ⓢ *Mon.–Sat.* 12–2.30pm, 8pm–midnight

The modest prices belie the quality of the cuisine in a restaurant that offers an unrivaled lunch menu. The warm atmosphere is as much due to a decor of natural stone and exposed beams as to the communicative enthusiasm of the proprietors. A clientele of regulars from the district's many publishing houses.

Paris (86)
43 boulevard Raspail, 75006 ☎ 01 49 54 46 90 ➡ 01 49 54 46 00

Ⓜ *Sèvres-Babylone* 🔼 *Gourmet cuisine* 🔲 ●●●● *à la carte* F450 ▨ Ⓢ *Mon.– Fri.* noon–2pm, 7.30–10pm; closed in Aug. and for 1 week in Feb. Ⓨ

The Paris is set in the 1930s decor of the only luxury hotel on the Left Bank – the Hôtel Lutétia ➡ 42. Philippe Renart's delightfully inventive cuisine is based on the availability of seasonal ingredients. Here, mushrooms, asparagus, truffles and baby vegetables are in the spotlight. Impressive chocolate dessert and a fine wine list.

Not forgetting

■ **Les Olivades (87)** 41 avenue de Ségur, 75007 ☎ 01 47 83 70 09 ● *Authentic Provençale cuisine re-created with feeling. The chef was born in Nîmes.* ■ **L'Œillade (88)** 10 rue Saint-Simon, 75007 ☎ 01 42 22 01 60 ●● *Simple cuisine, imaginatively prepared and full of flavor. Very reasonable prices.*

■ Where to shop ➡ 140 ➡ 156 ➡ 158

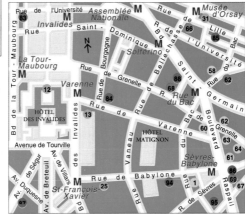

86

83

83

85

85

84

L'Arpège, situated between the National Assembly and the Hôtel Matignon, has an established clientele of political gourmets.

84

85

86

79

In the area

After World War I, Montparnasse became the preserve of artists and, later, of such writers as Ernest Hemingway, Jean-Paul Sartre and Simone de Beauvoir. Today, although the boulevard is monopolized by fast-food restaurants, the district still has a number of famous gourmet

Where to eat

Dominique (89)
19 rue Bréa, 75006 ☎ 01 43 27 08 80 ➡ 01 43 26 88 35

Ⓜ *Vavin* Ⓟ *Russian cuisine* ●●● *à la carte F200* ▭ Ⓘ *Mon. 7.15–11.30pm; Tue.–Fri. noon–2pm, 7.15–11.30pm; closed July 20–Aug. 20* ▦ *10am–2.30pm, 5.30–11.30pm*

Dominique is one of the last authentic restaurants of old Montparnasse, frequented by Russian princes and taxi drivers, which offers all the culinary splendors of Eastern Europe: *pirojki, chachliks,* eggplant caviar, beef Stroganoff and a wide range of vodkas. Managed by Françoise Dépée.

Le Caméléon (90)
6 rue de Chevreuse, 75006 ☎ 01 43 20 63 43 ➡ 01 43 27 97 91

Ⓜ *Vavin* Ⓟ *Bistro cuisine* ● *à la carte F200* ▭ Ⓘ *Mon.–Fri. noon–2pm, 8–10.30pm; Sat. 8–10.30pm; closed Aug. 1–15*

A real, old-fashioned Paris bistro where what is on your plate is more important than what is on the walls. For some time, the bar was one of the meccas of Montparnasse. The new proprietors are concentrating on the cuisine: lobster ravioli, home-made sausage and puréed potato, veal with fresh pasta. A good choice of light wines.

La Cagouille (91)
10 place Constantin-Brancusi, 75014
☎ 01 43 22 09 01 ➡ 01 45 38 57 29

(opposite 23 rue de l'Ouest) Ⓜ *Gaîté* Ⓟ *Seafood* ●●● *à la carte F260* ▭ Ⓘ *daily noon–2.30pm, 7.30–10.30pm*

Gérard Almendou was one of the inventors of all-fish cuisine. When asked whether this is a culinary style or fashion, he counters that it is simply the produce of the sea and rivers prepared with care and simplicity. Whatever it is, it has proved a huge success. The renovated, modern setting – in a district that is still trying to establish its identity – and the famous dishes (including a superb mussels dish) represent a particular type of modern cuisine.

Vin et Marée (92)
108 avenue du Maine, 75014 ☎ 01 43 20 29 50 ➡ 01 43 27 84 11

Ⓜ *Gaîté* ▨ *Seafood* ●●● ▭ Ⓘ *daily noon–3pm, 7.30pm–midnight* ▧ ▨

Vin et Marée, near the Gare Montparnasse, serves fish, shellfish and seafood amid 1930s decor. A promising new formula offered by an experienced team: good, simply prepared and inexpensive fish dishes served promptly and with a smile.

Not forgetting

■ **L'Opportun (93)** 64 boulevard Edgard-Quinet, 75014 ☎ 01 43 20 26 89 ●● *Simple dishes and modest regional wines in a bistro that is packed on market days.*

establishments. ■ Where to
eat ➡ 48 ➡ 66 ■ Where to
stay ➡ 44 ■ After dark ➡ 86

Seafood amid 1930s decor at the Vin et Marée (92),
or the more contemporary La Cagouille (91).

➡ **Where to eat**

Le Bamboche (94)
15 rue de Babylone, 75007 ☎ 01 45 49 14 40 ➡ 01 45 49 14 44

Ⓜ Sèvres-Babylone Ⓟ *Classic French cuisine* ●● *à la carte* F250 ▯ ⓧ
Mon.–Fri. noon–2.30pm, 7.30–11pm

Amid polished decor that does not disguise the origins of this modest workshop, the young chef David Van Laer creates an attractive culinary balance of seasonal products. This is first-class cuisine at bistro prices. You will have no cause for complaint, especially if you sample the pâté, the ox cheek in Graves or the stewed hare.

L'Épi Dupin (95)
11 rue Dupin, 75006 ☎ 01 42 22 64 56 ➡ 01 42 22 30 42

Ⓜ Sèvres-Babylone Ⓟ *Classic French cuisine* ● ▯ ⓧ *Mon.–Fri. 12.30–2.30pm, 7.30–10.30pm*

Spontaneous and uncomplicated cuisine offering low prices and high-quality ingredients. The extremely popular *capilotade d'agneau* (tiny pieces of lamb) wrapped in eggplant skins, and the *pain perdu* with fruit capture the mood of this cuisine with its subtle Mediterranean undertones.

Le Terroir (96)
11 boulevard Arago, 75013 ☎ 01 47 07 36 99

Ⓜ Les Gobelins **Good, plain cuisine** ●● *à la carte* F220 ▯ ⓧ Ⓧ *Mon.–Fri. noon–2.15pm, 7.45–10.15pm; Sat. 7.45–10.15pm*

Bright lights, yellow decor and just enough tables to create a convivial atmosphere. The *patron* places the emphasis on a few timeless dishes – ox muzzle in vinaigrette, *confit de canard* (filleted duck preserved in its own fat), potatoes *à la Sarladaise* (sautéed in goose fat) and the splendid guinea fowl with cabbage – which all call for carefully chosen wines.

La Régalade (97)
49 avenue Jean-Moulin, 75014 ☎ 01 45 45 68 58 ➡ 01 45 40 96 74

Ⓜ Alésia **Bistro cuisine** ●● ▯ ⓧ *Tue.–Fri. noon–2.30pm, 7.30pm–midnight; Sat. 7.30pm–midnight; closed July 15–Aug.15*

La Régalade is a dream come true – gourmet cuisine at affordable prices, courtesy of Yves Camdeborde, a native of the Béarn who trained in the top culinary schools. Although he decided on a bistro setting, his cuisine has other ideas. Even the all-pig platter – ear, snout and shoulder on a bed of braised cabbage – betrays the touch of a true chef. A warm and friendly welcome and an excellent choice of wines.

Not forgetting
■ **La Closerie des Lilas (98)** 171 boulevard du Montparnasse, 75006 ☎ 01 43 26 70 50 ●●●● *Typical brasserie dishes or Mediterranean cuisine created by the new chef.*
■ **La Verrière (99)** 10 rue du Général-Brunet, 75019 ☎ 01 40 40 03 30 ●● *Creative cuisine with classic overtones. Reasonably priced.*

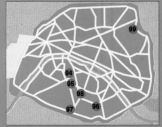

together to create an atmosphere of conviviality, soberly elegant decor, and a cuisine that makes use of simple, seasonal produce.

95

94

L'EPI DUPIN

97

98

After dark

Cash
Many Paris clubs, bars, theaters, etc. do not accept checks or credit cards.

Tips
A 15% service charge is always included, but keep change for attendants in movie theaters and concert halls. Tipping in national theaters ➥ 90 is prohibited.

Paris by night
The Bastille, Quartier Latin, Montmartre and Champs-Élysées are the capital's busiest districts at night.

Evening dress
Only cabaret theaters require customers to wear evening dress. Smart casuals are quite acceptable for the theater and opera.

Entertainment on a budget

Theater tickets are half price if bought on the day of the performance. Try the ticket kiosk in place de la Madeleine, or the one in front of Gare Montparnasse.

Entertainment guides

Two weekly publications give dates and times of evening entertainments.
Le Pariscope ● *F3* @ Pariscope.fr (includes a *Time Out* English section)
L'Officiel des Spectacles ● *F2*

44
Nights out

THE INSIDER'S FAVORITES

Advance booking

Shows: it is best to book at least 24 hours in advance.
Virgin Megastore 52 Champs-Élysées 75008
☎ *01 44 68 44 08* 🕓 *daily noon–midnight*
FNAC 136 rue de Rennes, 75006
☎ *01 49 87 50 50* 🕓 *Mon.–Sat 10am–7.30pm*
Clubs: telephone to avoid 'private party' evenings.

After dark

Virgin Café (1)
52–60 avenue des Champs-Élysées, 75008
☎ 01 42 89 46 81 ➡ 01 49 53 50 40

Ⓜ *Franklin-Roosevelt* Ⓟ ◷ *daily 10am–midnight* ● *F24–F47* ▣ ⊞ *11.30am–midnight* ◳ *3–7pm*

The café is on the top floor of the beautiful 1930s building currently occupied by the Virgin Megastore, and is strategically located at the top of the impressive staircase overlooking the store's vast record departments. Customers can sip their drinks, perched on a high stool or sitting comfortably on a chair designed by Philip Starck, and watch the latest promo videos before making their purchases.

Le Café de la Musique (2)
213 avenue Jean-Jaurès, 75019 ☎ 01 48 03 15 91 ➡ 01 48 03 15 18

Ⓜ *Porte-de-Pantin* Ⓟ ◷ *daily 8–2am* ● *F26–F55* ▣ ⊞ *11am–midnight* ♫ **Classical jazz** Wed. 10pm

It comes as no surprise that this beautiful café is an extension of the Cité de la Musique. Sit on velvet-covered chairs in soft, restful colors and sip delicious classic cocktails served against a background of world music. An atmosphere of quiet luxury pervades, with all the discreet sophistication of Parisian design by Élizabeth de Portzamparc.

Le Flore (3)
172 boulevard Saint-Germain, 75006
☎ 01 45 48 55 26 ➡ 01 45 44 33 39

Ⓜ *Saint-Germain-des-Prés* Ⓟ ◷ *daily 7–1.30am* ● *F23–F41* ▣ ⊞ ⊞ *26 rue Saint-Benoît: Mon. 2–8pm; Tue.–Sat. 11am–1pm, 2–8pm*

Since 1880 many well-known authors have frequented this discreetly charming and resolutely traditional café. It is still quite common to see literary prizewinners and celebrities savoring a perfect, if expensive, hot chocolate. Avoid weekends if you want to see it at its best.

Le Café de l'Industrie (4)
16 rue Saint-Sabin, 75011 ☎ 01 47 00 13 53 ➡ 01 47 00 92 33

Ⓜ *Bastille* ◷ *Sun.–Fri. 11–2am* ● *F10–F19* ▣ ⊞ *noon–midnight*

This old neighborhood café has been ingeniously renovated by its owner to preserve its original 1940s charm. This dedicated antique-hunter and traveler has collected the pictures, photographs, period frames and crocodile skins that cover the walls. Every picture tells a story.

Not forgetting
■ **Le Bar de l'Hôtel Raphaël (5)** 17 av. Kléber, 75116 ☎ 01 44 28 00 28 *Enjoy an aperitif in the intimate wood-paneled bar.* ■ **Le Fouquet's (6)** 99 avenue des Champs-Élysées, 75008 ☎ 01 47 23 70 60 *A rendezvous for those who want to see and be seen!* ■ **Le Dôme (7)** 108 boulevard Saint-Germain, 75014 ☎ 01 43 35 25 81 *Ideal for your first drink in a traditional Montparnasse café.*

beer) and drink it at the counter, at an inside table or on the terrace. Open from early morning through late at night – relax and watch the world go by.

Many Paris bars stay open into the early hours and some don't close until morning. The favorite haunts of Paris nightbirds include the Champs-Élysées, Boulevard Saint-Germain, Boulevard Montparnasse, Pigalle, Les Halles and Bastille. Most late-night bars provide

After dark

Le Floridita (8)

19 rue de Presbourg, 75116 ☎ 01 45 00 84 84 ⟶ 01 45 00 41 32

M *Charles-de-Gaulle-Étoile* 🔲 *Cigar bar* 🍴 🕒 *Mon.–Sat. 11–2am; Sun. 6pm–2am* ● *F15–F60* 🔲 🍴 *noon–3pm, 8pm–midnight*

Le Floridita, inspired by a bar of the same name in the Cuban capital of Havana, is devoted to cigar connoisseurs. Reddish-brown wood, wall hangings in dark green straw, soft lighting and wooden blinds create a restful and intimate atmosphere that has become the preserve of some very famous smoker. The cigars are reserved exclusively for customers and are stored in an unusual cellar: a bank strongroom!

Le Web Bar (9)

32 rue de Picardie, 75003 ☎ 01 42 72 57 47 ⟶ 01 42 72 66 75

M *Temple, République* 🅿 *Internet café* 🔲 🕒 *daily 11.30–2am* ● *F15; Internet F30/h* 🍴 *daily noon–3pm, 7pm–midnight* @ *webbar@webbar.fr*

The classic entrance to this former goldsmith's workshop offers no hint of what lies beyond. A metal and glass roof illuminates two floors of galleries devoted entirely to the Internet, where surfers of all persuasions can browse the Net. The first story has a comfortable lounge area with club chairs and concrete tables. Jazz and world music help to block out the clicking and beeping of the computers. An atmosphere of trendy sophistication.

Le China Club (10)

50 rue de Charenton, 75012 ☎ 01 43 43 82 02 ⟶ 01 43 43 79 85

M *Bastille* 🅿 🔲 🕒 *Le Fumoir Mon.–Thur. 7pm–2am; Fri.–Sat. 7pm–3am* ● *F60 Sing Song Fri.–Sat. 10pm–3am* ● *F50* 🔲 🍴 *daily 7pm–12.30am*

A haven of peace and quiet which combines French sophistication and colonial energy, and where you are assured of being in good company. Le China Club has three different types of atmosphere to suit your mood. Le Fumoir, with its quiet English-club atmosphere and open fire, is an ideal place to enjoy a pure malt whisky and a game of chess against a background of classical music. Or you may prefer a cocktail in the American bar, ensconced in a Chesterfield sofa or perched on a stool at the monumental mahogany bar, listening to 1940s jazz. The teahouse decor of the Sing Song offers a touch of glamour with its weekend jazz and blues concerts.

Not forgetting

■ **Le Moloko (11)** 26 rue Fontaine, 75009 ☎ 01 48 74 50 26
A modern bar with a friendly, lively atmosphere.
■ **Harry's New York Bar (12)** 5 rue Daunou, 75002
☎ 01 42 61 71 14 *Take a trip down memory lane. Harry's was a favorite meeting place for performers and intellectuals of the post-war period. American-style comfort in a discreet atmosphere.*
■ **La Casa del Habano (13)** 169 boulevard Saint-Germain, 75006
☎ 01 45 49 24 30 *A good menu with an opportunity to buy individual cigars.*

good-quality restaurant service
throughout the night.

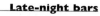

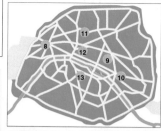

Basic facts

Paris has the largest number of theaters of any city in the world (276 in the city and suburbs) and performs the greatest number of plays (almost 1,000 per year). From the small private theaters (*théâtres de boulevard*) to the large, modern and heavily subsidized theaters, they

After dark

Théâtre national de Chaillot (14)
1 place du Trocadéro, 75116 ☎ 01 47 27 81 15

Ⓜ *Trocadéro* ☉ **Reservations** *10am–7pm* **Performances** *Tue.–Sat. 8.30pm; Sun. 3pm* ● *F160; under-18s, over-60s F120* 🚻 🎭 *Le Buffet* ♿ @ *culture.fr*

The Théâtre National Populaire (TNP), formed on November 11, 1920, moved into its permanent home in the Palais de Chaillot in 1938. Since then it has performed modern versions of classic works and helped to promote modern theater. Although it was renamed the Théâtre de Chaillot in 1972, it remains loyal to the image established by its unforgettable director, Jean Vilar. It combines a warm and friendly atmosphere with a high level of artistic and professional expertise. The Grand Foyer (main entrance hall) offers an unrivaled view of the Trocadéro gardens and the Eiffel Tower.

Odéon-Théâtre de l'Europe (15)
1 place Paul-Claudel, 75006 ☎ 01 44 41 36 36 ➡ 01 44 41 36 01

Ⓜ *Odéon* 🅿 ☉ **Reservations** *11am–6.30pm* **Performances** *Grande salle (main theater): Tue.–Sat. 8pm; Sun. 3pm* ● *F30–F150; Petit Odéon: Mon.–Sat. 6pm* ● *F70* 🚻 ▶️

Built in 1782 in the city center, this was the first Italian-style theater to provide seats in the stalls. Although twice burned down and rebuilt, it has retained its sumptuous decor, resplendent with gilt and moldings, magnificent red-carpeted staircases, prestigious boxes with scarlet hangings and a ceiling by André Masson (1965). Since the 1960s, its repertoire has tended to focus on Europe, but Europe did not feature in the title until 1990. Performances are on a par with the magnificent surroundings and are enhanced by excellent acoustics. The Odéon offers a truly unique dramatic experience.

Théâtre national de la Colline (16)
15 rue Malte-Brun, 75020 ☎ 01 44 62 52 52 ➡ 01 44 62 52 90

Ⓜ *Gambetta* ☉ **Reservations** *Tue.–Sat. 11am–7pm* **Performances** *variable* ● *F160; students, over-60s F130* 🚻 ▶️ 🎭

The modern vocation of this theater (opened in 1988) was maintained brilliantly and with great enthusiasm by its former director, Jorge Lavelli. Its huge façade – several stories of glass and colored tubes – reflects its performances which are both daring and unusual, and use the full range of dramatic creativity. In addition, its two theaters are very comfortable and offer an almost panoramic view of the stage. Before and after performances, the audience can enjoy a drink or dine in the art deco bar which is also used by the actors.

Not forgetting

■ **Théâtre de l'Olympia (17)** 28 boulevard des Capucines, 75009 ☎ 01 47 42 25 49 *A former music hall which today presents a wide variety of artists and performers.* ■ **Théâtre national de la Comédie-Française (18)** 2 rue de Richelieu, 75001 ☎ 01 44 58 15 15 *Founded in 1680 by Louis XIV, the Comédie-Française is the most traditional of the French theaters. It presents a repertoire of some ten French classics in rotation.*

have an extremely varied
repertoire in a wide variety of –
often unusual – styles.

ODEON
THEATRE DE L'EUROPE

15

COMÉDIE FRANÇAISE
1680
∗

COMÉDIE·FRANÇAISE

THÉÂTRE
DU VIEUX·
COLOMBIER

Saison
19 96
97

THÉÂTRE
NATIONAL
DE LA
COLLINE

16

16

Chai
llot !

DIRECTION JÉROME SAVARY

14

91

Basic facts

From classical music, ballet and opera to rock music and variety shows, the range of musical performances is as wide and varied as the theaters in which they are staged. The Parisian 'meccas' of music include two opera houses (the Garnier and the Bastille), the city's former cabaret

After dark

Théâtre des Champs-Élysées (19)
15 avenue Montaigne, 75008 ☎ 01 49 52 50 50 ➡ 01 49 52 07 41

M *Alma-Marceau* **P** *Concerts, opera, ballet* 🕐 *Reservations* 10am–noon, 2–6pm *Performances* times vary ● F50–F690 ▢ **Y** 🍴 *Maison Blanche* ➡ 48

This theater was founded in 1913 at the instigation of Gabriel Astruc and in response to a very real need. At the time, France had no large theater devoted to contemporary music. This modern building, which combines German architectural techniques, English comfort and French art (in the form of frescos by Antoine Bourdelle ➡ 122 and Maurice Denis ➡ 130), was described by Marcel Proust as a 'Temple of Music, Art and Architecture'. Since it opened, it has played a leading role in the world of music, with such composers as Claude Debussy, Camille Saint-Saëns and Gabriel Fauré directing their own works.

La Cigale (20)
120 boulevard Rochechouart, 75018
☎ 01 49 25 89 99 ➡ 01 42 23 67 04

M *Pigalle* **P** *Concerts, theater* 🕐 *Reservations* Mon.–Sat. noon–7pm *Performances* times vary ● F80–F200 ▢ **Y**

Since 1887, this cabaret theater has presented an amazing combination of French singing stars (e.g. Arletty, Maurice Chevalier) and futuristic plays by such writers as Jean Cocteau. It was converted into a movie theater before once again becoming a theater in 1987 through the impetus of the French theater company Les Rita Mitsouko. Updated with a modifiable auditorium and redecorated by Philip Starck, the new Cigale is always on the lookout for anything and anyone of interest, from avant-garde performances (like the famous Stomp) to established stars.

Opéra Bastille (21)
120 rue de Lyon, 75012 ☎ 01 44 73 13 99 ➡ 01 40 01 25 40

M *Bastille* **P** *Opera, concerts* 🍴 🕐 *Reservations* Mon.–Sat. 11am–6pm *Performances* variable ● F110–F610 ▢ **Y** 🎫 *01 40 01 19 70* @ *opera-de-paris.fr*

The Opéra Bastille was built, on this symbolic site, to commemorate the bicentenary of the French Revolution. The sweeping curves of the purpose-built structure are transformed at nightfall, when the light from inside the building shines out through the glass façade and shows the quality of the architecture to its best advantage. The vast interior is light and spacious, with pear wood, black velvet and sculptures by Niki de Saint-Phalle and Yves Klein contributing to an overall impression of comfort, humor and elegance. A perfectly balanced light emanates from the ceiling of the Grande Salle (main auditorium), which has a seating capacity of 2,700.

Not forgetting

■ **Salle Pleyel (22)** 252 rue du Faubourg-Saint-Honoré, 75008 ☎ 01 45 61 53 00 *A modern theater with excellent acoustics.*
■ **Palais Garnier (23)** 8 rue Scribe, 75009 ☎ 01 44 73 13 99 *A magical, legendary theater and an absolute must… if you manage to reserve seats.*

theaters (which offer old-fashioned charm yet may be filled with the latest in modern sound), and the concert halls with their often eclectic programs.

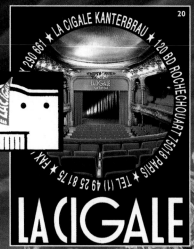

93

Basic facts

Paris has no less than 112 movie theaters. Movie-goers can choose from the avant-garde and experimental movie theaters of the Latin Quarter, or the commercial movie theaters of Montparnasse, the Champs-Élysées, Les Halles and Odéon. Paris also prides itself on having two of

After dark

Le Grand Rex (24)
1 boulevard Poissonnière, 75002 ☎ 08 36 68 70 23

🅜 *Bonne-Nouvelle* 🔳 🕐 *varies daily* ● ***Grande Salle*** *Mon. F36;Tue.–Sun. F46* ***Petite salle*** *Mon. F30;Tue.–Sun. F40* 📧 🎫 *08 36 68 05 96* ***double ticket (film and visit)*** *Wed., Sat., Sun. 10am–7.30pm* ● *F65* 🔰

In 1932, the Paris smart set celebrated the opening of Europe's largest movie theater, with its art deco façade, a magnificent entrance hall decorated with palm trees, Spanish haciendas and Venetian palaces, a seating capacity of 3,300 and – at the time – the world's biggest screen. Although this splendidly kitsch movie theater was later converted into seven smaller studios, the Grande Salle (main studio) has retained all its original magic: a 'ceiling' consisting of a star-studded vault some 65 ft high, an even bigger screen (336 sq yds) inaugurated in 1988, and a special Christmas show consisting of *La Féerie des eaux* (a water extravaganza) followed by the latest Walt Disney film.

La Pagode (25)
57bis rue de Babylone, 75007 ☎ 01 45 55 48 48 ➠ 01 45 50 33 79

🅜 *Saint-François-Xavier* 🕐 *daily 1pm–midnight* ● *Thur.–Tue. F47, under-12s F32;Wed. F38* 🔳 🔳 *Mon.–Sat. 4–9.45pm; Sun. 2–8pm* ⭐

La Pagode is not just a name, it is a genuine pagoda imported from Japan and rebuilt brick by brick. It was opened as a mainly avant-garde and experimental movie theater in 1927 and rapidly became the meeting place of such authors and film directors as Jean Renoir, Luis Buñuel and Jean Cocteau. Today its range may be wider but its atmosphere has remained unchanged: somewhere between that of a local movie theater and a movie club. You can even go there for tea or to walk in its exotic garden.

Gaumont Grand Écran Italie (26)
30 place d'Italie, 75013 ☎ 01 45 80 86 78 ➠ 01 45 80 86 87

🅜 *Place d'Italie* 🅿 🕐 *Sun.–Fri. 1pm–midnight; Sat. 1pm–2.30am* ● *F45–F53; over-60s F37–F44; under-12s F33* 🔳

This ultra-modern aluminum and monochrome glass building by Kenzo Tange is the city's very latest movie theater. One of its three studios has a truly amazing screen (290 sq yds) and a seating capacity of 652. The audience has a unique audio-visual experience due to the double-system and digital-sound projection equipment. The films shown in this studio are, of course, of the more spectacular variety. Not recommended for lovers of literary films.

Not forgetting

■ **Max Linder (27)** 24 boulevard Poissonnière, 75009 ☎ 01 48 24 88 88 *This movie theater is its own movie star, of the 1930s vintage. Wonderful decor, comfort, luxury and, of course, a big screen!* ■ **Kinopanorama (28)** 60 avenue de la Motte-Picquet, 75015 ☎ 01 43 06 50 53 *The 'Kino', with its wide, curved screen (18 yds long) has been a cult movie theater for generations of movie-goers from Paris, the rest of France and other countries!*

the largest screens in Europe –
one at the Gaumont Grand
Écran Italie, and the other at Le
Grand Rex.

25

25

24

26

26

24

95

Paris still has some of its legendary clichés: music halls, cabarets, the cancan and its famous revues. Although most date from the end of the 19th century, their names and music still fire the imagination. The districts of Montmartre, Pigalle, the Champs-Élysées and Montparnasse

After dark

Le Bal du Moulin Rouge (29)
82 boulevard de Clichy, 75018 ☎ 01 46 06 00 19 ➡ 01 42 23 02 00

M *Place-Blanche* 🚇 🍴 🕐 ***Performances*** daily 9pm, 11pm ● F510, F450
Performance & dinner daily 7pm ● F750–F880 ☐ 🍸 ● F240

It was the English who christened the high-kicking dance performed at the opening (1889) of the Bal du Moulin Rouge the 'French cancan'. Over one hundred years after La Goulue, the famous dancer immortalized by the posters of Toulouse-Lautrec, and after such great performers as Mistinguett, Josephine Baker, Édith Piaf, Maurice Chevalier and Yves Montand, the Moulin Rouge is still renowned for its lively atmosphere, its variety shows, its *joie de vivre*, its ability to amaze and its extremely talented performers.

Le Lido (30)
116bis avenue des Champs-Élysées, 75008
☎ 01 40 76 56 10 ➡ 01 45 61 19 41

M *George-V* 🅿 🍴 🕐 ***Performances*** daily 10pm, midnight ● F365, F540
Performance & dinner daily 7.30pm ● F770–F990 ☐ 🍸 ● F70–F240

To celebrate its 50th anniversary, Le Lido 'touched up its make-up' and presented its 25th revue: *C'est Magique!* Of course, there were plenty of feathers and Bluebell girls. These 60 famous dancers, handpicked for their remarkable physique and classical dance training, perform a truly spectacular musical extravaganza worthy of the third millennium. With the help of laser projection, digital laser sound and other technological devices, the dancers take the audience through a series of four tableaux: a giant video game, an aerial ballet, a gambling inferno and onto the ice of a huge skating rink.

Crazy Horse (31)
12 avenue George-V, 75008 ☎ 01 47 23 32 32 ➡ 01 47 23 48 26

M *Alma-Marceau* 🅿 🍴 🕐 ***Performances*** daily Sun.–Fri. 8.30pm, 11pm; Sat. 7.30pm, 9.45pm, 11.50pm ● F220–F560 ☐ 🍸 ● F100 @ crazy-horse.fr

Since 1951, Crazy Horse has been famous worldwide for its amazing nude performances. In an atmosphere of elegance and sophistication, 'the art of the nude' is embodied both on and off stage, as dancers perform the sequences from their latest revue – *Teasing* – to the eternal delight of the audience!

Paradis Latin (32)
28 rue Cardinal-Lemoine, 75005 ☎ 01 43 25 28 28 ➡ 01 43 29 63 63

M *Cardinal-Lemoine* 🅿 🍴 🕐 ***Performances*** Wed.–Mon. 9.45pm ● F465
Performance & dinner Wed.–Mon. 8pm ● F680 ☐

The framework of the Paradis Latin, built for the Paris Exhibition in 1889, was designed by Gustave Eiffel. As well as its spectacular revues in which a company of talented young dancers perform the wildly fantastical *Ville Lumière* (City of Light), it is also famous for its brigade of 25 waiters who are at your service to make this a truly memorable night out in Paris.

are traditionally associated with *Paris by night!*

29
30
31
32

31

30

32

Feathers, diamanté, choreography and champagne in *Paris by night*.

29

30

The history of French jazz is closely linked to modern political history. Jazz was introduced into France by the Americans during World War II. Cellars, soundproof and naturally protected, proved to be ideal venues for jam sessions and concerts. The habit stuck and the city's cellars and

After dark

Baiser Salé (33)
58 rue des Lombards, 75001 ☎ 01 42 33 37 71 ➡ 01 42 36 24 40

Ⓜ *Châtelet, Les Halles* Ⓟ *Latin, Afro, funk, blues, jazz* 🕐 *Mon.–Fri. 7.30pm–6am; Sat.–Sun. 3pm–6am* ● *F28–F49 Concerts 10pm* ● *F30–F50* ▭

Since it opened in 1983, this cellar club has presented every kind of jazz. This was world music ahead of its time! The club's eclectic approach is reflected in its comfortable setting and relaxed atmosphere. You feel immediately at ease among a clientele of all ages, styles and nationalities who share a common passion for jazz!

Duc des Lombards (34)
42 rue des Lombards, 75001 ☎ 01 42 33 22 88 ➡ 01 40 28 98 52

Ⓜ *Châtelet* Ⓟ *European jazz* 🕐 *Tue.–Sat. 6.30pm–3am Concerts times vary* ● *F70–F100* ▭ @ *actua.com/Duc-Des-Lombards*

The Duc des Lombards has broken with the tradition of Saint-Germain-des-Prés in more ways than one. Not only is it on the Right Bank, it isn't in a cellar! Between velvet furnishings and wood paneling, poster-covered walls trace the history of jazz. The program is just as innovative, with the club always on the lookout for modern European jazz.

La Villa (35)
29 rue Jacob, 75006 ☎ 01 43 26 60 00 ➡ 01 46 34 63 63

Ⓜ *Saint-Germain-des-Prés* Ⓟ *American jazz* 🍴 🕐 *Mon.–Sat. 6pm–2am* ● *Mon.–Fri. F120; Sat.–Sun. F150* ▭ 🏨

La Villa has occupied the magnificent vaulted cellars of the modern Villa Saint-Germain hotel ➡ 40 since 1991. Its carefully designed and soberly elegant decor creates a muted atmosphere in which a sophisticated clientele listens to top-quality jazz played by American-led 'combos'.

Le Petit Journal (36)
71 boulevard Saint-Michel, 75005
☎ 01 43 26 28 59 ➡ 01 43 54 30 17

Ⓜ *Luxembourg, Cluny* Ⓟ *New Orleans jazz* 🕐 *Mon.–Sat. 11–2am, closed Aug.* ● *F100* ▭ 🏨

Le Petit Journal only opened in 1971, but its comfortable 1950s atmosphere gives the impression that it has been around much longer. Located in Saint-Germain-des-Prés, in the heart of the Latin Quarter, its exceptional program makes it one of the meccas of New Orleans jazz. Regulars include Claude Bolling, Marcel Zanini, Claude Luter and Benny Bailey.

Not forgetting

■ **Hot Brass (37)** Parc de La Villette, 211 avenue Jean-Jaurès, 75019 ☎ 01 42 00 14 14 *In the heart of La Villette, with an eclectic program of contemporary jazz and world music.* ■ **New Morning (38)** 7–9 rue des Petites-Écuries, 75010 ☎ 01 45 23 56 39 *An absolute must for jazz lovers – memorable performances on stage and from the floor.*

basements still house most of its swing and jazz clubs.

34

33

37

36

Paris nightbirds have a taste for themes and artistic directors are having to use their imagination and ingenuity to devise impressive theme evenings. For example, a 'snow' or 'tropical' evening involves covering the dance floor with 'snow' or hot sand. Admission is usually free for

After dark

Les Bains (39)
7 rue du Bourg-l'Abbé, 75003 ☎ 01 48 87 01 80 ➡ 01 48 87 13 70

M *Étienne-Marcel* ☉ *daily 11.30pm–5am* ● *Mon.–Fri. F100; Sat., Sun. F140* ▯
Y ⌂ *daily 9pm–5am*

Walking through the attractive wrought-iron gate and up the steps of these converted, early 20th-century public baths, doesn't necessarily mean you will get in. This fashionable venue has a marked preference for celebrities from the movie, press and fashion world. The easiest way to get in is to reserve a table in the restaurant: the cuisine – French – is sophisticated, and the original decor is often enhanced by an exhibition of photographs or paintings. From there, you can go straight on to the dance floor. Once you are there, it won't matter whether the pool is covered or open, empty or full, whether the atmosphere is tropical or freezing, or the music funk or techno. You'll simply be glad to be there!

Le Balajo (40)
9 rue de Lappe, 75011 ☎ 01 47 00 07 87 ➡ 01 47 00 09 69

M *Bastille* P ☉ *Tue.–Fri. 11.30pm–6am; Sat., Sun. 3–7pm; 11.30pm–6am* ●
Tue.–Fri. F100; Sat., Sun. F50 ▯ Y

In 1936, the 'Bal à Jo' opened with a performance by the famous Mistinguett. It was an unmitigated success and the Paris smart set flocked to dance to the sound of accordion music, the traditional accompaniment in the popular dance halls of Paris. Although the music

women, provided they are suitably dressed: après-ski or swimwear only!

has changed – fresh-disco or house music, depending on the night's theme – the atmosphere is still much the same. Le Balajo's clientele of committed and indefatigable young dancers can enjoy the convivial atmosphere as they dance on a traditional parquet floor amid period decor.

La Casbah (41)
18–20 rue de la Forge-Royale, 75011
☎ 01 43 71 71 89 ➠ 01 43 71 63 42

M *Faidherbe-Chaligny* **P** **◷** *8pm–6am* ● *Sun.–Thur. F80; Fri., Sat. F120* **□** **⊞**
Sun., Tue.–Fri. 8–11.30pm; Sat. 8pm–3am

The 'Arabian Nights' decor of this Moroccan club is evident in wrought-iron gates, heavy carved-wood doors, mosaic floors and crystal-clear fountains. Customers can sample the restaurant's spicy, gourmet cuisine before being swept up by the oriental languor and intoxicating rhythms (ranging from soul to 1980s) of the dance floor. The club's comfortable bench seats, 1930s chairs, multicolored cushions, frescos and paintings are enjoyed by a cosmopolitan clientele.

Not forgetting

■ **La Locomotive (42)** 90 boulevard de Clichy, 75018 ☎ 01 53 41 88 88 *Each story (including a 'machine room') in this club is in a different style.*
■ **Chez Castel (43)** 15 rue Princesse, 75006 ☎ 01 43 26 90 22
➠ 01 40 51 72 74 *Once the city's trendiest disco, today this famous private club on the Left Bank is full of memories.* ■ **Niel's (44)** 27 avenue des Ternes, 75017 ☎ 01 47 66 45 00 *Popular with the show-business and fashion worlds.*

What to see

Special rates
30–50% reductions for children, students, senior citizens, groups.
Free admission for minors in 65 Paris museums and monuments.
Carte Musée et Monuments (museums and monuments card) Offers a saving if you plan to visit several sights. ● F65 (1 day); ● F140 (2 days); ● F200 (5 days). Available from museums, métro stations and tourist offices.

Underground Paris
Catacombs *Place Denfert-Rochereau 75014* ☎ *01 43 22 47 63*
Ⓜ *Denfert-Rochereau* 🕐 *Tue.–Fri. 2–4pm; Sat.–Sun. 9–11am, 2–4pm* ● *F27*
Paris sewers *Quai d'Orsay 75014* ☎ *01 47 05 10 29* Ⓜ *Alma-Marceau*
🕐 *Sat.–Wed. 11am–5pm* ● *F25*

Boat trips on the Seine

Bateaux parisiens Tour Eiffel ☎ *01 44 11 33 44* Ⓜ *Trocadéro*
Bateaux parisiens Notre-Dame ☎ *01 43 26 92 55* Ⓜ *Saint-Michel*
Vedettes du Pont-Neuf ☎ *01 46 33 98 38* Ⓜ *Pont-Neuf*
Bateaux Mouches ☎ *01 40 76 99 99* Ⓜ *Pont de l'Alma*

47
Sights
THE INSIDER'S FAVORITES

Information

Tourist Office *127 av. des Champs-Élysées, 75008* ☎ *01 49 52 53 54*
Museums Association *25 rue du Renard, 75004* ☎ *01 44 78 45 81*
Paris Leisure Service ☎ *01 47 20 94 94* (24 hours)

Basic facts

Built in the early 13th century as a fortress, the Louvre became a
Renaissance palace during the reign of François I (1515–47). Merged with
the 16th-century Palais des Tuileries in 1868, it was converted into a
museum (1793), and extended and renovated between 1981 and 1993.

▶ What to see

Musée du Louvre (1)
34–36 quai du Louvre, 75001 Paris ☎ 01 40 20 50 50

Ⓜ *Palais-Royal, Louvre* ▬ Ⓨ *Antiquities, paintings, sculpture, objets d'art,
graphic art* Thur.–Sun. 9am–5.30pm; Mon.,Wed. 9am–9.30pm; closed public
holidays **Hall Napoléon** Mon.,Wed.–Sat. 9am–10pm **History of the Louvre**
Wed.–Mon. 10am–9.45pm ● before 3pm F45; after 3pm; Sun. F26; under-18s,
1st Sun. of the month free 🟨 🔲 🏛 🎫 🚻

The Musée du Louvre is divided into three
main wings (named Denon, Sully and Richelieu)
which can be reached from the Hall Napoléon
on the first story of the famous glass pyramid
(designed by I. M. Pei). The museum's
extensive and magnificent collections, put
together since the reign of François I, include
the art of ancient civilizations, as well as
western art from the Middle Ages to 1850. The
Musée du Louvre is a huge museum, and rather than
trying to see everything superficially, it is better to
concentrate on a particular period in greater depth.
For example: Egypt (Sully, *salles* – i.e. rooms – Charles X); French
sculpture from the Early Middle Ages to the 19th century (Richelieu,
salles 1–33); the Northern French Schools from the 15th–17th century
(Richelieu, *salles* 3–39); the French School 18th–19th century (Sully,
salles 36–73). Three paintings in particular attract large numbers of
visitors: Leonardo da Vinci's *Mona Lisa* (1503–06) (Denon 8, *salle* 5),
Théodore Géricault's *Raft of the Medusa* (1819) (Denon 8, *salle* 77)
and Jan Vermeer's *Lacemaker* (Richelieu 2, *salle* 38).

Musée de l'Orangerie (2)
Jardin des Tuileries, place de la Concorde, 75001 ☎ 01 42 97 48 16

Ⓜ *Concorde* 🚻 Ⓢ *Mon., Wed.–Sun. 9.45am–5.15pm; closed public holidays* ●
F30; 18–25s F18; under-18s free 🔲 🏛.

Two Second-Empire buildings – the Musée de l'Orangerie and the Galerie
du Jeu de Paume – flank the entrance to the Jardin des Tuileries, on the
place de la Concorde. Since 1977, the former orangery of the Palais des
Tuileries has housed the Walter-Guillaume collection, consisting of
almost 150 paintings dating from 1870 to 1930. It includes
masterpieces by Cézanne, Renoir, Picasso, Matisse, Utrillo,
Soutine, Derain and Modigliani. Eight magnificent water lily
compositions by Monet are displayed in two basement rooms.

Galerie du Jeu de Paume (3)
Place de la Concorde, 75001 ☎ 01 47 03 12 50

Ⓜ *Concorde* 🚻 Ⓢ *Tue. noon–9.30pm; Wed.–Fri. noon–7pm; Sat.–Sun.
10am–7pm* ● *F38; 13–18s, over-60s F18; under-13s free* 🔲 📷 🏛
bookshop

This former royal-tennis court (*jeu de paume*), built during
the reign of Napoleon III, was renovated in 1931. Since 1991,
it has housed temporary exhibitions of modern art.

2

Not forgetting

▬ **Musée des Arts Décoratifs (4)** Palais du Louvre, 107 rue de Rivoli,
75001 ☎ 01 44 55 57 50 Ⓢ Tue.–Sun. noon–6pm; closed public holidays.
220,000 pieces from the Middle Ages to the 20th century.

An impressive vista stretches from place de la Concorde to place Charles-de-Gaulle-Étoile and on to the Grande Arche of La Défense.
■ Where to stay ➡ 18 ➡ 20 ➡ 22 ■ Where to eat ➡ 50 ➡ 52 ➡ 56 ➡ 74 ■ After dark ➡ 86 ➡ 88 ➡ 90

What to see

Arc de Triomphe (5)
Place du Général-de-Gaulle, 75008 ☎ 01 43 80 31 31

Ⓜ *Charles-de-Gaulle-Étoile* Ⓟ ▣ Ⓒ *Oct.–Mar.; Sun.–Mon. 10am–6pm, Tue.–Sat. 10am–10.30pm; Apr.–Sep.: Sun.–Mon. 9.30am–6.30pm, Tue.–Sat. 9.30am–11pm; closed Dec. 25* ● *F35; 12-25s F23; under-12s free* 🔾 🔾

From its position in the center of place Charles-de-Gaulle-Étoile, the Arc de Triomphe offers a magnificent view of the Champs-Élysées. Built between 1806 and 1836, it is the symbol of the Napoleonic era. Beneath the archway, the tomb of the Unknown Soldier makes it a place of remembrance also. A small museum traces the history of the monument.

Musée de la Mode et du Costume (6)
Palais Galliéra, 10 av. Pierre-1ᵉʳ-de-Serbie, 75015 ☎ 01 47 20 85 23

Ⓜ *Iéna* ▣ Ⓒ *Tue.–Sun. 10am–5.40pm* ● *temporary exhibitions (vary)* 🔾

The Museum of Fashion and Costume is a pleasantly unusual museum. It traces the development of French society from 1735 through the history of fashion. And what better setting than the former palace of the Duchesse de Galliéra for its 30,000 costumes and 70,000 accessories?

Musée d'Art Moderne (7)
11 avenue du Président-Wilson, 75016 ☎ 01 53 67 40 00

Ⓜ *Iéna* ▣ Ⓒ *Tue.–Fri. 10am–5.30pm; Sat.–Sun. 10am–6.45pm; closed public holidays* ● *F27; concessions F19; double ticket Museum-Exhibitions F40; concessions F30* ▣ 🔾

This temple of contemporary art was opened in 1961 in the Palais de Tokyo (1937). It features the Fauvist paintings of Matisse and Dufy, the Cubist works of Braque and Picasso, sculptures by Lipchitz and Zadkine, and the more recent works of Parisian and other European artists.

Tour Eiffel (8)
Champ-de-Mars, 75007 ☎ 01 44 11 23 45

Ⓜ *Champ-de-Mars* ▣ Ⓒ *Sep. 1–June 12: daily 9.30am–11pm; June 13–Aug. 30: daily 9am–midnight* ● **Lift** *Level 1: F20; under-12s F10; Level 2: F42; under-12s F21; Level 3: F57; under-12s F28* **Stairs** *Levels 1 and 2: F14* 🔾 🔾 *Altitude 95 (Level 1); Le Jules Verne* ➡ *50 (Level 2)* ▣ *Poste* 🔾

The Eiffel Tower, designed by Gustave Eiffel (1832–1923), was chosen from among 107 projects for the 1889 Paris Exhibition. The 984-foot tower – raised to 1052 feet in 1959 – is today the world-famous symbol of Paris. Magnificent views of the capital from Level 3.

Not forgetting
■ **Musée national des Arts asiatiques-Guimet (9)** 6 place d'Iéna, 75116 ☎ 01 47 23 61 65 Ⓒ Wed.–Mon. 9.45am–5.45pm; closed on public holidays. *Museum closed until Sep. 1999, but the Émile Guimet collections can be seen at the Hôtel Heidelbach (19 av. d'Iéna, 75116)* ■ **Musée de l'Homme (10)** Palais de Chaillot, 17 place du Trocadéro, 75116 ☎ 01 44 05 72 72 Ⓒ Wed.–Mon. 9.45am–5.15pm; closed public holidays.

Map labels:

N↑

Av. de la Gde-Armée

Rue de Ch.-de-Gaulle Étoile

R. Le Sueur

8

5

Tilsitt

Avenue Foch

ARC DE TRIOMPHE

13 11

14

Rue de Presbourg

Hugo

Victor

Kléber

M

5

4

Av. Marceau

Rue

Avenue

Paul

Valéry

Viauriston

Av. Kléber

Rue d'Iéna

Avenue J. Giraudoux

Rue Copernic

Rue Boissière

21

Rue

Rue Kléber

Place des États-Unis

R. G. Bizet

M Boissière

R. St-Didier

72

Rue Boissière

Avenue d'Iéna

Avenue Kléber

11

25

23

9

Av. P. 1er de Serbie

Rue de Longchamp

6

9

Avenue d'Iéna

Avenue du Président Wilson

7

M Trocadéro

M Iéna

Av. d'Iéna

14 10

JARDINS DU TROCADÉRO

Nations-Unies

de New - York

Branly

Av. des

Bd Delessert

Avenue

Pont d'Iéna

TOUR EIFFEL

Quai

8 8

Champ-de-Mars

CHAMP-DE-MARS

M

7

10

In the area

The sweeping avenues of the Invalides and Grand Palais districts are laid out with military precision. They are bordered by mansions, embassies, government ministries, and museums housed in historic residences or in buildings built for the 1900 World Fair.

What to see

Petit Palais (11)
Avenue Winston-Churchill, 75008 ☎ 01 42 65 12 73

Ⓜ *Champs-Élysées-Clemenceau* ▣ 🕒 *Tue.–Sun. 10am–5.40pm; closed on public holidays* ● *F27; concessions F14.50; under-18s free* ▦ ▤

A baroque setting for an original concept in art. The Grand Palais and Petit Palais, two of the capital's major exhibition galleries, stand on either side of avenue Churchill, which runs between the Champs-Élysées and the Cours de la Reine. Both were built for the 1900 World Fair. The Petit Palais presents municipal art collections, including the bequest of the Dutuit family which ranges from Antiquity to 1925.

Invalides (12)
Esplanade des Invalides, 75007 ☎ 01 44 42 37 72

Ⓜ *Latour-Maubourg, Varenne* ▣ 🕒 **Musée de l'Armée, Musée de l'Ordre de la Libération, Dôme des Invalides, Napoleon's tomb** *Apr.–Sep.: daily 10am–6pm; Oct.–Mar.: daily 10am–5pm; closed public holidays* ● *F37; under-26s F27; over-60s, under-12s free* **Musée des Plans-Reliefs** *Apr.–Sep.: daily 10am–12.30pm, 2–6pm; Oct.-Mar.: daily 10am–12.30pm, 2–5pm* ▦

An essential visit for anyone interested in French military history, the Hôtel des Invalides was built during the reign of Louis XIV (1670–1706) as a convalescent home for wounded soldiers. Today it houses the Musée de l'Armée (Military Museum), whose collections trace the military history of France from its origins to the present day, and the Musée des Plans-Reliefs (Museum of Relief Maps), with models of fortified towns illustrating the art of siege, from Louis XIV to Napoleon III. The church of the Dôme contains the massive tomb of Emperor Napoleon I. The esplanade stretching between the Invalides and the Pont Alexandre III is one of the most beautiful in Paris.

Musée Rodin (13)
Hôtel Biron, 77 rue de Varenne, 75007 ☎ 01 44 18 61 10

Ⓜ *Varenne* 🅿 ▭ 🕒 *Tue.–Sun.: Apr.–Sep. 9.30am–5.15pm; Oct.–Mar. 9.30am–4.15pm; closed public holidays* ● *F28; Sun., concessions F18; under-18s free* ✪ *Tue.–Sun.: Apr.–Sep. 9.30am–6.45pm; Oct.–Mar. 9.30am–5pm* ● *F5* ▦ ▣ *in summer* ▤ 🛈 **Villa des Brillants** *19 avenue Auguste-Rodin, 92190 Meudon ☎ 01 45 34 16 09*

When sculptor Auguste Rodin died in 1917, his 17th-century residence was converted into a museum dedicated to his life and works. Its rooms and gardens house such monumental sculptures as *The Burghers of Calais*, *The Thinker* and *Balzac*, as well as works by his former student and mistress Camille Claudel, and paintings by Monet, Renoir and Van Gogh.

Not forgetting

■ **Palais de la Découverte** (14) avenue Franklin-Roosevelt, 75008 ☎ 01 40 74 80 00/01 40 74 87 82 **Planetarium** ☎ 01 40 74 81 73 🕒 *Tue.–Sat. 9.30am–6pm; Sun. 10am–7pm; closed public holidays Popularized science.* ■ **Grand Palais** (15) 3 avenue du Général-Eisenhower, 75008 ☎ 01 44 13 17 17 🕒 *Thur.–Mon. 10am–8pm; Wed. 10am–10pm; closed public holidays Temporary exhibitions.*

■ Where to eat ➡ 60 ➡ 78
■ Where to stay ➡ 22

Many of the city's major buildings are decorated with gold, chosen by the
monarchs of the Ancien Régime to symbolize faith, strength, durability and wealth.

The Marais, centered around place des Vosges, rue des Francs-Bourgeois and rue Saint-Antoine, is one of the few truly historic districts of Paris (16th–17th century). ■ Where to stay ➡ 32 ■ Where to eat ➡ 72 ■ After dark ➡ 86

What to see

Musée Picasso (16)
Hôtel Salé, 5 rue de Thorigny, 75003 ☎ 01 42 71 25 21

Ⓜ *Chemin-Vert, Saint-Paul* Ⓟ 🍴 ⏰ *Apr.–Sep.: Wed.–Mon. 9.30am–6pm; Oct.–Mar.: 9.30am–5.30pm; closed public holidays* ● *F38; 18–25s, Sun. F28; under-18s free* ☎ *01 42 71 70 84* ▦

The 17th-century Hôtel Salé is one of the most beautiful buildings in Paris. Since 1985 it has housed the works of Pablo Picasso (1881–1973). The development of Picasso's work, from 1905 through 1973, is traced via 203 paintings, including *Two women running on the beach* (1922), and *Self-Portrait* (1901), 158 sculptures, numerous reliefs, collages, ceramics and illustrated books, as well as 3000 drawings and engravings.

Hôtel de Soubise (17)
60 rue des Francs-Bourgeois, 75003 ☎ 01 40 27 60 96

Ⓜ *Rambuteau, Hôtel-de-Ville* Ⓟ 🍴 ⏰ ***Musée de l'Histoire de France*** *Wed.–Tue. noon–5.45pm; closed public holidays* ● *F15; concessions F10; under-18s free* ▦ ***National archives*** ☎ *01 40 27 60 00* ⏰ *Tue.–Sat. 9am–6pm*

An ideal place to learn about the history of France. In 1808, Napoleon I chose the magnificent 18th-century Hôtel de Soubise to house the national archives. Since then, they have spread into the Hôtel de Rohan and four other neighboring mansions and currently occupy around 280 miles of shelving. The most original documents in the archives are on display in the Musée de l'Histoire de France (Museum of French History) which is open to the general public.

Musée Carnavalet (18)
Hôtel Carnavalet, 23 rue de Sévigné, 75003 ☎ 01 42 72 21 13

Ⓜ *Saint-Paul, Chemin-Vert* Ⓟ 🍴 ⏰ *Tue.–Sun. 10am–5.30pm; closed public holidays* ● *F27; 18–25s F14.50; under-18s free* ☎ ▦ *bookshop*

A truly magnificent setting in which to learn about the history of the French capital. The museum consists of two neighboring mansions linked by a passageway. The first is the beautiful Hôtel Carnavalet of Madame de Sévigné, which combines Renaissance and classical styles and provides the setting for the history of Paris from the Middle Ages to the 18th century. The second, the mansion of Le Pelletier de Saint-Fargeau, traces the history of the capital from the Revolution (1789) to the present day. The collections (paintings, engravings, models, sculptures, furniture and signs) are presented in rooms that re-create the atmosphere of Parisian mansions from different historical periods.

Not forgetting

■ **Centre Georges Pompidou ('Beaubourg') (19)** 19 rue Beaubourg, 75004 ☎ 01 44 78 12 33 ⏰ Mon., Wed.–Fri. noon–10pm; Sat., Sun., public holidays 10am–10pm (renovations to end 1999) *Exhibitions and events in all spheres of modern art.* ■ **Hôtel de Béthune-Sully (20)** 62 rue Saint-Antoine, 75004 ☎ 01 44 61 20 00 ⏰ Heritage bookshop: Tue.–Sun. 10am–7pm ☎ Guided visits only (☎ 01 44 61 21 69) *Magnificent 17th-century mansion, painstakingly restored.*

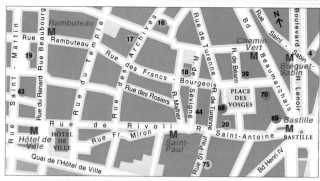

The Pompidou Center, a steel-and-glass modernist structure, attracts 8 million visitors every year.

In the area

Montmartre, a former wine-growers' village that became part of the capital in 1860, looks out across Paris from the top of its famous *butte* (hill). From the place du Tertre, a haunt of artists, a maze of steep streets and steps leads down to the *grands boulevards*. ■ Where to eat ➡ 64

What to see

Musée de Montmartre (21)
12 rue Cortot, 75018 ☎ 01 46 06 61 11

Ⓜ Abbesses ▣ ◐ *Tue.–Sun 11am–6pm; closed public holidays* ● F25; concessions F20; under-10s free ▣ ▦

The museum, housed in the *butte*'s oldest building (1650), was originally a private residence whose occupants have included artists (Dufy, Utrillo, Renoir) and poets (Reverdy). Its collections (posters, paintings and porcelain) reflect Montmartre's 'Bohemian period'. The Café de l'Abreuvoir and the studio of 19th-century composer Gustave Charpentier have been reconstructed.

Basilique du Sacré-Cœur (22)
33 rue du Chevalier-de-la-Barre, 75018 ☎ 01 53 41 89 00

Ⓜ Anvers ◐ **Basilica** *daily 7am–11pm* ● *free* **Dome, crypt** *daily: Apr.–Oct. 9am–7pm; Nov.–Mar. 9.30am–6pm* ● F15 each ▦ ▨

The white dome of the Sacré-Coeur, dominating the Paris skyline from the *butte* of Montmartre, is one of the city's most famous landmarks. Built (1876–1910) in combined Romanesque and Byzantine styles, the basilica was originally intended for pilgrimages.

Musée Gustave Moreau (23)
14 rue de la Rochefoucauld, 75009 ☎ 01 48 74 38 50

Ⓜ Trinité ▣ ◐ *Mon., Wed. 11am–5.15pm; Thur.–Sun. 10am–12.45pm, 2–5.15pm* ● F22; Sun., 18–25s F13; under-18s free ▦ ▣ *1st and 3rd Wed. in the month*

The museum, devoted to the work of the French symbolist Gustave Moreau (1826–1898), was founded in the artist's studio in 1902. A collection of almost 1200 paintings (including *Jupiter and Semele*) and 5000 drawings presents a cohesive overview of Moreau's work. The Petit Musée in the artist's apartment offers a more personal view of his life.

Musée Grévin (24)
7 boulevard Montmartre, 75009 ☎ 01 47 70 85 05

Ⓜ Rue-Montmartre, Richelieu-Drouot ℙ ▣ ◐ *daily 1–7pm; school holidays 10am–7pm* ● F55; 6–14s F36; under-6s free ▦

This world-famous waxworks museum, opened in 1882, was the brainchild of journalist Arthur Meyer and cartoonist Alfred Grévin. A series of tableaux features several hundred waxwork models of famous historical figures and contemporary celebrities. The Palais des Mirages presents a *son et lumière*, while the Italian-style theater (which became a listed building in 1964) stages mime performances and magic shows.

Not forgetting

■ **Passage Jouffroy (25)** 10 boulevard Montmartre, 75002 *The city's first heated alleyway.* ■ **Passage des Panoramas (26)** 11 boulevard Montmartre, 75002 *The city's oldest alleyway, described by Émile Zola (1840–1902) in his novel Nana.*

22

Built on a hill undermined
by quarrying, Sacré-Coeur
is supported by 83 under-
ground pillars. According
to locals, the basilica holds
Montmartre together.

23

In the 19th century, working-class districts grew up around the former villages of La Villette and Belleville, and along the banks of the Ourcq and Saint-Martin canals. During the 1870s, the abattoirs of La Villette closed down and its population migrated into the suburbs, significantly altering

What to see

Cité des Sciences et de l'Industrie (27)
Parc de la Villette
30 avenue Corentin-Cariou, 75019 ☎ 01 40 05 70 00

Ⓜ *Porte-de-La-Villette* Ⓟ ▣ Ⓞ *Cité des Sciences, Planetarium Tue.–Sat. 10am–6pm; Sun. 10am–7pm* ● *F50; concessions F35; under-7s free* 🅱 *Cité des Enfants Tue., Thur., Fri. 11.30am, 1.30pm, 3.30pm; Tue., Sat., Sun. 10.30am, 12.30pm, 2.30pm* ● *F20 Techno cité* ● *F25 Cinaxe Tue.–Sun. 11am–7pm* ● *F34; concessions F29 Géode Tue.–Sun. 10am–9pm F57; concessions F44* 🈳 Ⓨ ▣ 🈵 *L'Aquarium*

The largest museum of modern science and technology in Europe offers additional attractions (planetarium, aquarium, introduction to technology, submarine visit). The Géode movie theater, a steel globe that houses the world's largest hemispherical screen, has become the symbol of the Cité. In the landscaped gardens are the Cité de la Musique, Grande Halle and Hot Brass ➡ 98.

Parc des Buttes-Chaumont (28)
Place Armand-Carrel, 75019 ☎ 01 42 40 88 66

Ⓜ *Botzaris, Buttes-Chaumont* Ⓞ *Park daily 7.30am–10.45pm (7pm in winter) Guignol (puppet show) Apr.–Oct.: Wed., Sat., Sun. public holidays, school holidays 3pm, 4pm* ● *F12* 🈳 🌿

Created in 1867 by the civil engineer Jean-Charles Alphand, this was the archetype for the parks built during Georges Eugène Haussmann's period of office as prefect of Paris (1853–1870). It was laid out during the reign of Napoleon III to encourage working-class families to take Sunday walks rather than visit cabarets. It has a waterfall, two streams, a cave and a lake. The Temple de Sybille stands at the highest point on the island and offers a magnificent view of northern Paris.

Musée Édith Piaf (29)
5 rue Crespin-du-Gast, 75011 ☎ 01 43 55 52 72

Ⓜ *Ménilmontant* Ⓞ *Mon.–Thur. 1–6pm by appointment* ● *free* 🈳 🅱

The first museum to be dedicated to a French variety artist evokes the life and career of the popular singer Édith Piaf (1915–1963), née Édith Giovanna Gassion. Among the many memorabilia presented in this intimate museum is the famous 'little black dress' worn on stage by the singer affectionately known as 'the Little Sparrow'.

Père Lachaise Cemetery (30)
Boulevard de Ménilmontant, 75020 ☎ 01 43 70 70 33

Ⓜ *Père-Lachaise, Philippe-Auguste* Ⓞ *Mar. 16–Nov. 5: Mon.–Sat. 7.30am–6pm; Sun. 9am–6pm; Nov. 6–Mar. 15: Mon.–Sat. 8.30am–5pm; Sun. 9am–5pm* 🅱

A maze of – often eccentric – tombs inscribed with such famous names as Molière, La Fontaine, Proust, Balzac, Colette, Jim Morrison… As well as the tombs, there is the *Mur des Fédérés*, the wall against which the last of the Communards (the supporters of the Paris Commune formed after the Franco-Prussian War in 1871) were executed in 1871, and memorials to the victims of the Nazi concentration camps.

the face of the Paris 'east-end',
a process that continues.

■ Where to eat ➡ 48 ➡ 50
■ After dark ➡ 86 ➡ 90 ➡ 98

La Rotonde, a former
toll-house used by tax
collectors to administer
the city toll. Built in 1784
by the architect Claude
Nicolas Ledoux
(1736–1806).

Centered on the Musée d'Orsay, this district includes the Hôtel de la Monnaie (Mint), the Institut de France, the École des Beaux-Arts (School of Fine Arts) as well as art galleries and antique shops. ■ Where to stay ➡ 38 ➡ 40 ➡ 42 ■ Where to eat ➡ 78 ■ After dark ➡ 86 ➡

What to see

Musée d'Orsay (31)

62 rue de Lille, 75007 ☎ 01 40 49 48 14
(entrance: 1 rue de Bellechasse)

Ⓜ *Solférino* Ⓞ *Sep. 21–June 19:Tue.–Wed., Fri.–Sat. 10am–5.45pm,Thur. 10am–9.30pm, Sun. 9am–5.45pm; June 20–Sep. 20:Tue.–Wed., Fri.–Sat. 9am–5.45pm,Thur. 9am–9.30pm ● F39; 18–25s F29; under-18s free;* **double ticket** *Museum-Exhibitions F55* 🖾 🖾 *Le Café des Hauteurs* 🍴 *Le Restaurant* 🖾 🖾
☎ *01 45 49 11 11*

The museum occupies the for Gare d'Orléans, built on the of the Palais d'Orsay, which v burned to the ground during th Paris Commune in 1871. In 1900 the Orléans Railway Company built a new station, designed by the architect Victor Laloux (1850–1937). The station ceased operating in 1939 and remained empty for several decades. It was subsequently used as a sale room by Hôtel Drouot, the famous Paris auction house, and then as a theater by the Renaud-Barrault company before being saved from demolition in 1973 and converted into a museum in 1986. The luminous hall of the former station forms the central 'nave' of the museum, around which the collections are presented on terraces and mezzanines.

88 ➡ 98
■ Where to
shop ➡ 156

19th-century art

The collections of the Musée d'Orsay reflect western art from 1848 to 1914. They have been formed from national collections from three principal sources: the Louvre ➡ 104, the Jeu de Paume ➡ 105 and the Musée d'Art Moderne ➡ 106. The originality of the Musée d'Orsay lies in its presentation of a wide range of different art forms from a particularly fertile period. This gives a complete overview of painting, sculpture, decorative and graphic arts, as well as such visual arts as architecture and urban development, movies, photography, posters and book illustrations.

Paintings

The museum is organized chronologically on three levels, with rooms generally devoted to the work of one artist. Paintings are grouped according to theme and school. The museum possesses one of the finest collections of Impressionist paintings in the world (level 3), including Édouard Manet's *Olympia* (1863), Claude Monet's *La Cathédrale de Rouen: harmonie bleu et or, plein soleil* – one of the Rouen Cathedral 'series' – (1893), Renoir's *The Swing* (1876) and works by Pissarro and Sisley. However, it also gives an insight into modern art via the Naturalist (level 2) (Edgar Degas's *La Famille Bellelli*, 1860), Expressionist (Vincent Van Gogh's *La Nuit étoilée, Arles*, 1888), Pointillist (Paul Signac's *Femme à l'Ombrelle*, 1893), Nabi (level 3) (Pierre Bonnard's *La Loge*, 1908) and early Cubist (Paul Cézanne's *Le Pont de Maincy*, 1879) schools.

Not forgetting

■ **L'Hôtel des Monnaies (32)** 11 quai de Conti, 75006 ☎ 01 40 46 55 35 ◑ Tue.–Sun. 11am–5.30pm *Engraving, medal manufacture and casting of objets d'art.* ■ **L'Église Saint-Germain-des-Prés (33)** 3 place Saint-Germain-des-Prés, 75006 ☎ 01 43 25 41 71 ◑ Mon.–Sun. 7.30am–7.30pm ▣

In the area

The Île de la Cité constitutes the historic and geographical center of Paris. Notre-Dame, the Sainte-Chapelle, Hôtel Dieu (rebuilt in the 19th century) and Conciergerie are all that remain of the former royal city. The Pont Neuf offers superb views of the island. ■ Where to eat ➡ 76

What to see

Conciergerie (34)
Palais de la Cité, 1 quai de l'Horloge, 75001 ☎ 01 53 73 78 50

Ⓜ *Saint-Michel, Cité* Ⓞ *daily: Apr.–Sep. 9.30am–6.30pm; Oct.–Mar.: 10am–5pm; closed public holidays* ● *F32; 12–25s F21; under-12s free:* **double ticket** *Conciergerie-Sainte-Chapelle F50* 🔲 🔳 *daily 11am, 3pm*

Originally the prison of the Capetian palace built on the northern shore of the island in c.1300 by Philippe le Bel (1268–1314). In 1380, it became an annexe of the Grand Châtelet prison. The Salle des Gens d'Armes (room of the men-at-arms) houses several pieces from this period. Many famous prisoners were detained here pending execution, especially in 1793 during the French Revolution. A visit to the Prisoners' Gallery, the dungeons and the cell of Queen Marie-Antoinette (converted into a chapel in 1816) gives some insight into these troubled times.

Sainte-Chapelle (35)
4 boulevard du Palais, 75001 ☎ 01 53 73 78 50

Ⓜ *Saint-Michel, Cité* Ⓞ *daily: Apr.–Sep. 9.30am–6.30pm; Oct.–Mar. 10am–5pm; closed public holidays* ● *F32; 12–25s F21; under-12s free* 🔲 🔳 *daily 11am, 3pm*

Sainte-Chapelle, a real jewel of Gothic architecture which today stands within the walls of the Palais de Justice (Law Courts), used to stand in the main courtyard of the Palais de Saint-Louis. Built (1245–1248) as a royal shrine to house holy relics, it comprises two chapels, a lower chapel for the public and an upper chapel for the king. The absence of flying buttresses, which have been replaced by buttresses, made it possible to increase the size of the windows. Their fragile delicacy is accentuated by the relatively small dimension of the building and a very tall spire (250 feet). The windows illustrate the history of the Hebrew people, from the Creation to their arrival in Israel and the institution of a monarchy; they end with the story of Louis IX receiving the relics of the Passion.

Notre-Dame de Paris (36)
place du Parvis-de-Notre-Dame, 75004 ☎ 01 42 34 56 10

Ⓜ *Cité* Ⓞ **Cathedral** *Sun.–Fri. 8am–6.45pm; Sat. 12.30–2pm* **Towers** *daily: Dec.–Jan. 10am–4pm; Feb.–Mar. 10am–5pm; Apr.–Sep. 9.30am–6.30pm; Oct.–Nov. 10am–5pm* ● *F15; concessions F10; under-12s F5* 🔳 **Treasure-house** *Mon.–Sat. 9.30am–5.30pm* ● *F15; concessions F10; under-12s F5* **Crypt** *Apr.–Sep. 10am–5.30pm; Oct.–Mar. 10am–4.30pm* ● *F32; 12–25s F21; under-12s free* 🔲

This magnificent Gothic cathedral (1163–1245) took more than 150 years to build. The sober harmony of its impressive bulk provides a striking contrast to its slender spire (295 feet) and the subtle balance of its flying buttresses. Among the interior details are the rose window in the north transept depicting scenes from the Old Testament, and the north and south walls (14th century) illustrating the *Life of Christ*. The towers (225 feet) offer a magnificent view of the city and such architectural details as the Galerie des Chimères with its gargoyles and monsters by Viollet-le-Duc (19th century). At the other end of the scale, the crypt, opened in 1980, enables visitors to see the cathedral's Gallo-Roman foundations.

■ Where to
stay ➡ 34 ➡
38 ■ Where
to shop ➡ 140

35

The bronze star in front of Notre-Dame
represents not only the heart of Paris,
but also the heart of France.

36

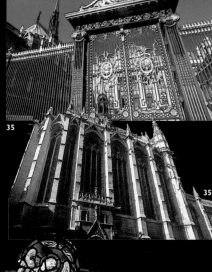

35

35

35

35

35

35

119

The universities, publishing houses and bookstores of the Latin Quarter have established its reputation as the intellectual center of Paris. It also offers a blend of monuments and medieval streets that are busy day and night. ■ Where to eat ➡ 48 ➡ 76 ■ Where to stay ➡ 34 ➡ 36

What to see

Hôtel de Cluny and Thermal Baths (37)
Musée national du Moyen Âge
6 place Paul-Painlevé, 75005 ☎ 01 53 73 78 00

Ⓜ Cluny-La-Sorbonne ℗ 🔁 🕒 Wed.–Mon. 9.15am–5.45pm ● F30; 18–25s F20; under-18s free 🚻 🎫 Music and medieval poetry ☎ 01 53 73 78 30

The Museum of the Middle Ages, founded in 1843, spans 15 centuries of history. The remains of its first- to third-century Gallo-Roman baths and the 16th-century mansion (hôtel) of the abbots of Cluny (a masterpiece of the Flamboyant style) make the museum the architectural embodiment of this period. The richness and diversity of medieval life is evidenced in the museum's sculptures, manuscripts, paintings and windows. The famous 16th-century tapestry, Lady with the Unicorn, is one of the museum's masterpieces.

Institut du Monde Arabe (38)
1 rue des Fossés-Saint-Bernard, 75236 Cedex ☎ 01 40 51 38 38

Ⓜ Jussieu, Cardinal-Lemoine ℗ ➖ 🕒 Tue.–Sun. 10am–6pm; closed May 1 ● F25; concessions F20; under-18s free Library Tue.–Sat. 1–8pm Image and sound Tue.–Sun. 1am–6pm 🎫 🚻 🍴 🎿

Discover the Arab world via the Institut du Monde Arabe (IMA), founded in 1987. Its permanent collections are enhanced by regular exhibitions of large collections from the Institute's founder countries, while its print library (50,000 books) and multimedia reference library provide additional information on the civilizations and cultures of the Arab world.

Muséum National d'histoire Naturelle (39)
57 rue Cuvier, 75005 ☎ 01 40 79 30 00

Ⓜ Censier-Daubenton 🔁 🕒 Grande Galerie de l'Évolution (Gallery of Evolution) Wed., Fri.–Mon. 10am–5pm; Thur. 10am–10pm ● F40; concessions F30 🎫 Paleontology, anatomy and mineralogy Oct.–Mar.: Wed.–Mon. 10am–5pm; Apr.–Sep.: Mon., Wed.–Fri. 10am–6pm; Sat., Sun. 10am–6pm ● F30; concessions F20 🎫 Entomology Mon.–Fri. 1–5pm; Sat., Sun. 10am–6pm ● F15; concessions F10 Menagerie Mon.–Sat. 1–5pm; Sun., public holidays 10am–6pm ● F30; concessions F20 🅿 Gardens daily, sunrise to sunset

Set in the Jardin des Plantes, this natural history museum was established in 1793. Its collections of natural history and ethnology are today among the largest in the world. Visit the late 19th-century Grande Galerie de l'Évolution with its huge glass roof, the gallery of paleontology with its reconstructed skeletons of prehistoric mammals, the botanical gardens and the menagerie.

Not forgetting

■ **Panthéon (40)** Place du Panthéon, 75005 ☎ 01 40 51 75 81 🕒 Apr.–Sep.: daily 10am–6pm; Oct.–Mar.: daily 10am–5pm "Aux Grands Hommes, la Patrie reconnaissante." (The mother land pays homage to its great men.)
■ **Arènes de Lutèce (41)** 49 rue Monge, 75005 🕒 daily 10am–5.30pm Beautiful Gallo-Roman amphitheater discovered in 1869.

37 The Flamboyant ceilings of the Hôtel de Cluny chapel exemplify the final stylistic development of French Gothic architecture.

38

39

39

38

Green spaces have always been an important part of Paris life: the former private parks and formal gardens of the 17th-century royal and princely palaces, the public gardens of the 18th century, and the Bois de Boulogne and the Bois de Vincennes developed during the Second

What to see

Jardin du Luxembourg (42)
Boulevard Saint-Michel, 75006

Ⓜ *Odéon* 🕓 *daily 9am–sunset free* ● *free* 🎫 *Puppet theater, hives* 📷 ✳

The Jardin du Luxembourg was created at the same time as the palace built for Queen Maria de' Medici (17th century), today the seat of the French Senate. Together with the Jardin des Tuileries, it is one of the oldest gardens in Paris, designed by the first exponent of the French-style garden, Boyeau de la Bareaudière. Today children play around the garden's huge, ornamental pool and enjoy its puppet theater, and it is also a favorite rendezvous for students and residents of the Latin Quarter. The shady walkways offer glimpses of 19th-century sculptures (Cain, Bourdelle, Frémiet), including the fountain dedicated to Eugène Delacroix and decorated with a bronze sculpture by Jules Dado, and the famous Medici fountain.

Parc Monceau (43)
Boulevard de Courcelles, 75008 ☎ 01 42 27 08 64

Ⓜ *Courcelles* 🕓 *daily Apr.–Oct.: 7am–9.45pm; Nov.–Mar.: 7am–7.45pm* ● *free*

Created in 1778 by the Duc de Chartres, this park has the magical charm of an English-style garden. With ornamental pools, grottoes, mock Gothic ruins and ruined Greek temples, and statues of Musset (Antonin Mercié, 1906), Maupassant (Verlet, 1897) and Chopin (Froment-Meurice, 1906), the park is as popular with children as it is with adults. Near the north entrance, La Rotonde (built by Ledoux in 1784) is one of the oldest toll-houses used by tax collectors to administer the city toll. The park – a particular favorite of Marcel Proust – is surrounded by mansions, two of which house the Musée Cernuschi (Chinese art) and the Musée Nissim-de-Camondo (18th-century decorative arts).

45

45

42

Empire. The tradition continues, and today the capital has some 400 parks, private and public gardens and local squares.

Parc André-Citroën (44)
rues Balard, Leblanc, Montagne-de-la-Fage, 75015 ☎ 01 45 57 13 35

Ⓜ *Balard* ◯ *Mon.–Fri. 7.30am–sunset; Sat., Sun. 9am–sunset* ● *free*

Parc André-Citroën was created by landscape designers Alain Provost and Gilles Clément, in the mid-1970s, on the site of the Citroën factories. It is probably the most sophisticated of the Paris parks and comprises the Jardin Blanc (white garden), used for games and walking, the Jardin Noir (black garden) with its dense, dark-colored plantings, and the large central park which descends toward the Seine. A series of six gardens, separated by waterfalls, completes the transformation of the site.

Not forgetting

■ **Jardin du Musée Bourdelle (45)** 18 rue Antoine-Bourdelle, 75015 ◯ Tue.–Sun. 10am–5.40pm *Garden-museum of Bourdelle sculpture.*
■ **Parc Montsouris (46)** av. Reille, 75013 ◯ daily, sunrise–sunset *English-style garden.* ■ **Jardin des Tuileries (47)** Le Louvre ➡ *104*
◯ *daily, Apr.–Sep. 7am–9pm; Oct.–Mar. 7.30am–7.30pm A French-style garden created by Le Nôtre in 1666.* ■ **Parc des Buttes Chaumont (28)**
A picturesque garden. ➡ *114.*

45

43

42

Cycle hire

Some railway stations hire bicycles that can be returned to another station ● *F45 per day* **SNCF** ☎ *01 45 82 50 50*

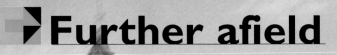

Further afield

Rambles

Organized by the Paris ramblers' association: **Randonneurs d'Île-de-France** *67 rue du Moulin-Vert, 75014* ☎ *01 45 42 24 72*

Information

SNCF 24 hours ☎ *01 40 52 75 75* et **36 15** *SNCF*
RATP 24 hours ☎ *08 36 78 77 14* et **36 15** *RATP*
Paris leisure service 24 hours ☎ *01 47 20 94 94*

17
Days out

THE INSIDER'S FAVORITES

Festivals and events around Paris

Versailles ➡ 128 Concerts in Opéra Royal of the Château de Versailles *(Feb.–July)*; Grandes Fêtes de Nuit *(June 29–July 6)*; Grandes Eaux Musicales *(Aug. 31–Sep. 7)*
Chantilly ➡ 132 Equestrian displays at the Musée Vivant du Cheval, Cheval & Gospel, Cheval & Fête *(Feb.–Nov.)*; Nuits de Feu, international fireworks competition *(mid-June)*
Saint-Denis ➡ 132

Religious dance and music *(June)*
Fontainebleau ➡ 134 Week of the Horse at the Grand Parquet hippodrome *(July)*
Barbizon ➡ 134 Prix de Peinture (art prize) *(Oct.)*
Thoiry ➡ 136 Rhododendron and azalea festival *(May–June, Oct.)*; Rose and peony fortnight *(June)*
Golf national ➡ 136 French Open *(end of June)*

Basic facts

The forests around Paris were once royal hunting grounds. Today they are occupied by chateaux and museums for the culturally and historically minded, parks for visitors in search of fresh air, golf courses for sports enthusiasts and huge theme parks for the younger generation.

Further afield

Musée Maurice Denis (7)

🚗 *(45 min)*
Autoroute A13 to Versailles-Ouest exit; RN186 in the direction of Saint-Germain-en-Laye.
RER *(35 min)* Line A1 to Saint-Germain-en-Laye.

Château de Chantilly (10)

🚗 *(75 min)*
Autoroute A1 to Survilliers-Saint-Witz exit; RN16 in the direction of Chantilly.
RER *(45 min)* Line D to Chantilly-Gouvieux.

Château de Versailles (1)

🚗 *(45 min)*
Autoroute A13 to Versailles exit.
RER *(30 min)* Line C to Versailles-Rive-Gauche.
🚆 *(30 min)* gare Saint-Lazare, to Versailles-Rive-Droite.
🚆 *(20 min)* gare Montparnasse, to Versailles-Chantiers.

Château d'Écouen (9)

🚗 *(60 min)*
Autoroute A1 to Pierrefitte-Beauvais exit; RN1 and RN 16 in the direction of Chantilly.
🚆 *(25 min)* gare du Nord, to Écouen-Ezanville, bus no. 268 alighting at Mairie d'Écouen.

Château de Saint-Germain-en-Laye (6)

🚗 *(45 min)*
Autoroute A13 to Versailles-Ouest exit; RN 186 in the direction of Saint-Germain-en-Laye.
RER *(35 min)* Line A1 to Saint-Germain-en-Laye.

Château de la Malmaison (5)

🚗 *(45 min)* RN 13 dir. Saint-Germain-en-Laye.
Ⓜ *(20 min)* Line 1 to La Défense; bus no. 258, to Le Château station (5 min walk from the château).

Château et parc de Thoiry (15)

🚗 *(45 min)*
Autoroute A13; A12 to Bois-d'Arcy exit; RN 12 in the direction of Dreux. At Pontchartrain, take the RD (or D) 11 to Thoiry.

Musée National de la Céramique (4)

🚗 *(45 min)* in the direction of porte de Saint-Cloud.
Ⓜ *(35 min)* Line 9 to Pont de Sèvres.

Golf National (17)

Ⓜ *(40 min)*
Autoroute A13, A12 and then the A12A to Guyancourt exit.

Basilique Saint-Denis (8)

🚗 *(20 min)*
Autoroute A1 to Saint-Denis exit.
Ⓜ *(25 min)* Line 13 to Saint-Denis-Basilique.

Saint-Germain-en-Laye

A1

15
Thoiry

D11

RN12

RN10

17
Golf Natio

Château de Fontainebleau (13)

🚗 *(90 min)*
Autoroute A6 to Fontainebleau exit.
🚆 *(40 min)* gare de Lyon to Fontainebleau-Avon, bus 'AB' to the chateau (15 min).

7

15

1

9

Senlis

Chantilly 10

D924a

16
Parc Astérix

A16

RN1

RN16

D922

RN17

A1

9 **Écouen**

Roissy -
Ch. de Gaulle ✈

Parc Astérix (16)

🚌 *(60 min)*
*Autoroute A1 to
Parc Astérix exit.*
RER *(40 min) Line
B, Station Roissy-
Charles-
de-Gaulle 1. Fare-
paying shuttle (20
min).*

Seine

A14

RN13

**Saint-
Denis**
8

A104

5 **Rueil-
Malmaison**

PARIS

A86

RN34

Disneyland Paris 14

Marne-la-Vallée

4 **Sèvres**

Versailles

A4

A86

Disneyland
& Golf (14)

🚌 *(45 min)*
*Autoroute A4 to
Parc Disneyland
Paris exit.*
RER *(45 min) Line
A 4, station Marne-
la-Vallée-Chessy.*

Château de
Vaux-le-
Vicomte (11)

🚌 *(60 min)*
*Autoroute A6 to
Melun-Sénart exit.*

✈
Orly

A10

A6

A104

RN7

Barbizon (12)

🚌 *(50 min)*
*Autoroute A6 to
Fontainebleau exit
in the direction of
Barbizon.*

Vaux-le-Vicomte 11

Melun

A5

Seine

RN37

RN2

Barbizon 12

A6

Fontainebleau
13

RN6

16

13

It took 100 years and four royal reigns to build this impressive royal palace. Louis XIII's passion for hunting dictated the site, and the aspirations of Louis XIV, the Sun King, decided its vast size. Louis XV brought intimacy and elegance, and Marie-Antoinette added youthful

▶ Further afield

Château de Versailles (1)
78000 Versailles ☎ 01 30 84 76 18

May–Sep.: Tue.-Sun. 9am–6pm; Oct.–Apr.: Tue.-Sun. 9am–5pm ● F45; 18–25s F35; under-18s free; Museums and Monuments Card **Galeries historiques du XVIIe siècle-Galeries des Batailles** open intermittently. Concerts in the **Opéra Royal ☎** 01 39 02 30 00 La Flottille

Built between 1661 and 1710 by Le Vau and decorated by Le Brun, Versailles is a fine example of classical architecture, with its buildings and wings arranged symmetrically around the main body of the chateau. In 1678, for reasons of politics and prestige, Louis XIV took up residence at Versailles along with the royal family, the royal Court and the French government. The chateau was extensively modified so that a strict hierarchy could be observed in the allocation of apartments. The North (1689) and South (1682) wings housed the princes and nobility. The royal apartments were located in the main chateau, with the queen's apartments to the south and the king's magnificent and lavishly ceremonial Grand Appartement to the north. The elegant sophistication of the Petits Appartements, commissioned by Louis XV, offer a striking contrast. Don't miss the Opéra, commissioned by Louis XVI and designed by Gabriel, or the famous Hall of Mirrors lined by 17 windows and 17 arcaded mirrors.

Gardens and Grand Canal (2)

daily 7am–sunset ● admission free (except during Grandes Eaux) **Grandes Eaux Musicales** May–Oct. 15 ● F25 **Grandes Fêtes de Nuit** June–Sep. ☎ 01 39 50 36 22

Designed by Le Nôtre and embellished by Mansart, the park of Versailles provided the setting for some lavish celebrations and entertainments. At the foot of the chateau are the 'open' gardens whose broad, sweeping vistas are punctuated by terraces and ornamental pools. Beyond these lie the groves, garden rooms furnished with almost 300 ornamental basins and statues. The majestic Grand Canal draws the eye into the distance, where the park merges with the vast forest of Versailles.

frivolity. King Louis-Philippe gave it to the nation as a museum.

Allée du Rendez-vous
Bd Saint-Antoine

HAMEAU
DE LA REINE

GRAND
TRIANON **3** PETIT
TRIANON

Boulevard de la Reine

A

Av. de Trianon

Avenue de
Saint-Cloud

GRAND CANAL

1

2

Av. de Paris
ÉCURIES

CHÂTEAU
DE VERSAILLES

Route de Saint - Cyr

RN10

Under Louis XIV, the Grand Canal provided the setting for lavish entertainments.

Le Grand et le Petit Trianon (3)

🕐 May–Sep.:Tue.–Sun. 10am–6pm; Oct.–Apr.:Tue.–Sun. 10.0am–12.30pm,
2–5.30pm ● *Grand Trianon* F25; 18–25s, Sun. F15; under-18s free;
Museums and Monuments Card ⊞ ● *Petit Trianon* F15;
18–25s, Sun. F10; under-18s free; double ticket Grand-Petit
Trianon F30; 18–25s F20; under-18s free

The long Italianate building of the Grand Trianon (1887) and the neoclassical residence known as the Petit Trianon (1762) were Louis XIV's and Louis XV's favorite parts of the chateau. Marie-Antoinette made Trianon her own domain and added the Hameau de la Reine (queen's hamlet). This reconstruction of a farm enabled her to enjoy the pleasures of 'rural' life, as advocated by writer Jean-Jacques Rousseau (1712–78). Centuries later, these 'miniature' palaces continue to delight visitors.

Not forgetting

■ **Les Trois Marches (A)** 1 boulevard de la Reine, 78000 Versailles
☎ 01 39 50 13 21 *Gastronomic restaurant.* ●●●●●

Basic facts
The Bourbon kings' passion for hunting meant that the court was
constantly traveling between the Palais du Louvre and Saint-Germain-en-
Laye, Vincennes and Saint-Cloud. This 'nomadic existence' came to an
end when Louis XIV took up residence at Versailles. Today, the former

Further afield

Manufacture Nationale de Porcelaine (4)
Musée national de la Céramique
Place de la Manufacture, 92310 Sèvres ☎ 01 41 14 04 20

📅 🕐 *Wed.–Mon. 10am–5pm; closed public holidays* ● *F22; concessions F15;
under-18s free; Musées et Monuments card* 🔲 🔳 ☎ *01 41 14 04 23*

It was the Manufacture Nationale de Porcelaine, on the edge of the park
of Saint-Cloud, that established the reputation of Sèvres porcelain in the
18th century. The museum, founded in 1824, has a collection of over
12,000 pieces, dating from the Renaissance to the present day. It includes
Italian majolica pottery, faience from Chantilly and Mennecy, porcelain
from Saxony and Sèvres, and contemporary pieces made in the factory.

Château de Malmaison (5)
Musée National de Malmaison-parc Bois-Préau
Avenue du Château, 92500 Rueil-Malmaison ☎ 01 41 29 05 55

📅 🕐 *Apr.–Sep. Mon., Wed.–Fri. 9.30am–12.30pm, 1.30–5.45pm; Sat., Sun.
10am–6.30pm / Oct.–Mar.: Mon., Wed.–Fri. 9.30am–12.30pm, 1.30–5.15pm; Sat.,
Sun. 10am–6pm* ● *F30; Sun.–Sat., 18–25s F20; under-18s free; Musées et
Monuments card*

This 18th-century chateau stands in a magnificent English-style park
dotted with pavilions. It enshrines the memory of Napoleon Bonaparte
and Joséphine de Beauharnais, for whom it was built. It became a
national museum in 1906. Don't miss the library, still in its original form.

Château de Saint-Germain-en-Laye (6)
Musée des Antiquités nationales
Place du Château, 78103 Saint-Germain-en-Laye ☎ 01 34 51 53 65

📅 🕐 *Wed.–Mon. 9am–5.15pm* ● *25 F; 18–25s F17; under-18s free; Musées et
Monuments card* 🔳 🔲

From royal fortress (12th century) to Renaissance palace (16th century),
the chateau refurbished by Louis XIV became a museum in 1862. It is the
richest prehistoric museum in the world, with collections that span a
million years. One of its finest exhibits is the reconstruction of the Grotte
de Lascaux (Dordogne).

Musée Maurice-Denis – Le Prieuré (7)
2bis rue M. Denis, 78100 Saint-Germain-en Laye ☎ 01 39 73 77 87

📅 🕐 *Wed.–Fri. 10am–12.30pm, 2–5.30pm; Sat., Sun. 10am–12.30pm,
2–6.30pm; closed public holidays* ● *F25; concessions F15; under-12s free; Musées
et Monuments card* 🔲

In 1914, this former royal general hospital (1680) was bought by Maurice
Denis (1870–1943), a leading artist in the symbolist Nabi group. In 1980,
'Le Prieuré' became a museum devoted to the works of Denis and
other 19th- and 20th-century artists.

Not forgetting
■ **Cazaudehore (B)** 1 avenue du Président-Kennedy, 78100
Saint-Germain-en-Laye ☎ 01 34 51 93 80 *Gastronomic cuisine.* ●●●

hunting-grounds exist as parks, offering spectacular views of the city, as well as unusual museums. Well worth a visit.

The *Dame de Brassempouy* (20,000 BC), discovered in south-west France, is exhibited in the Musée des Antiquités (6).

Three splendid buildings lie within easy reach of Paris to the north –
the Basilisue de Saint-Denis (the first major Gothic structure, and the
mausoleum of the kings of France), Château d'Ecouen (a 16th-century
chateau, now the setting for the Musée National de la Renaissance) and

► Further afield

Basilique de Saint-Denis (8)
2 rue de Strasbourg, 93200 Saint-Denis ☎ 01 48 09 83 54

Tombs-Crypt 🔲 🕐 *Apr.–Sep.: Mon.–Sat. 10am–7pm; Sun. 10am–12 noon,
5–7pm / Oct.–Mar.: Mon.–Sat. 10am–5pm; Sun. 10am–noon; closed during
religious services* ● *F32; 12–25s F21; under-12s free; Musées et Monuments card*
Festival of religious music and dance in June

The Basilique de Saint-Denis (1122), built on the site of a 5th-century
shrine housing the tomb of Saint Denis, became the prototype for later
French cathedrals. Consecrated as the royal mausoleum by Louis VI, it
houses the tombs of the kings of France, from Dagobert (d. 639) to
Louis XVIII (d. 1824). The royal sepulchers and recumbent statues in the
crypt trace the history of the nation's royal dynasties. The only museum
of funereal art of its kind in the world.

Château d'Écouen (9)
Musée National de la Renaissance, 95440 Écouen ☎ 01 34 38 38 50

🔲 🕐 *Wed.–Mon. 9.45am–12.30pm, 2–5.15pm; closed public holidays* ● *F25;
18–25s F17; under-18s free; Musées et Monuments card; Sun. F17* 🎨 🖼 *Sat.,
Sun.*

This magnificent building, built for Anne de Montmorency (1493–1567),
was converted into a museum (1969) at the instigation of the French
writer and minister for Cultural Affairs, André Malraux. Architectural
wealth and remarkable collections, are dominated by magnificent
Renaissance tapestries depicting the story of David and Bathsheba.
The park was designed by Jules Hardouin-Mansart.

Château de Chantilly (10)
60631 Chantilly ☎ 03 44 62 62 62

Musée Condé 🔲 🕐 *Mar.–Oct.: Wed.–Mon. 10am–6pm / Nov.-Feb.: Wed.–Mon.
10.30am–12.45pm, 2–5pm* ● *F39; 12–18s F34; 3–11s F12; under-3s free;
Musées et Monuments card* 🎨 🖼 *La Capitainerie* 🔲 *Musée Vivant du Cheval*
🔲 🕐 *Apr., July–Oct.: Wed.–Mon. 10.30am–6.30pm / May–June daily 10.30am–
6.30pm / Nov.-Mar.: Mon., Wed.–Fri. 2.–6pm; Sat., Sun., public holidays 10.30am–
6.30pm* ● *F50; under-16s F40; under-4s free* 🏛 🖼 *Le Carrousel Gourmand* 🎨

At the center of a vast estate, this chateau was converted into a museum
in 1886. The Petit Château (1560) houses the apartments of the princes
de Condé, while the Grand Château (1875–85) holds collections of
paintings (French School, Italian Renaissance, Northern French School)
and a magnificent library. The park, designed by Le Nôtre, includes the
Grand Canal, characteristically formal flowerbeds, an Anglo-Chinese
garden and the Grandes Écuries (1719), considered to be the most
beautiful stables in the world. They were converted into the Musée Vivant
du Cheval (living museum of the horse) in 1982. A trip in a hot-air
balloon enables visitors to appreciate this remarkable estate from above.

Not forgetting
■ **Mets du Roy (C)** 4 rue de la Boulangerie, 93200 Saint-Denis ☎ 01 48
20 89 74 *Traditional French cuisine* ●● ■ **Les Goûters Champêtres (D)**
Moulin du Hameau, 60500 Chantilly ☎ 03 44 57 46 21 *Regional cuisine* ●

Château de Chantilly (an imposing building, set in an extensive park, and which houses the art collection of the Musée Condé).

The equestrian displays at the Musée Vivant du Cheval are very popular.

The passion for hunting shared by most French monarchs led to the construction of hunting lodges on the edge of the vast game-filled forests of the Île-de-France region. This was how such royal residences as the Château de Fontainebleau were first established, while other

 # Further afield

Château de Vaux-le-Vicomte (11)
77950 Maincy ☎ 01 64 14 41 90

🔲 ⊙ *Mar., 1–Nov. 11: daily 11am–5pm; Apr.–Oct.: Mon.–Fri. 10am–1pm, 2–6pm; Sat., Sun., public holidays 10am–6pm* **Château-museum-gardens** ● F56; concessions F46; under-6s free **Gardens-museum** ● F30; concessions F24; under-6s free 🔲 🏛 ⊙ **Candlelit visits** May–Oct. 15: Sat. 8.30–11pm ● *F75; concessions F65; under-6s free*

This great 17th-century palace – commissioned by Fouquet, minister of finance to Louis XIV – was the work of architect Le Vau, interior designer Le Brun, and landscape designer Le Nôtre, all of whom were later to work for Louis XIV and XV. The sumptuous apartments painted by Le Brun are furnished with 17th-century furniture, and the tapestries are amongst the most beautiful in France. Glorious gardens by Le Nôtre, immaculately restored. Summer candlelit tours are well worth the effort.

Musée de l'École de Barbizon (12)
Auberge Ganne, 92 Grande-Rue, 77630 Barbizon ☎ 01 60 66 22 27

▬ ⊙ *Oct.–Mar.: Mon., Wed.–Fri. 10am–12.30pm, 2–5pm; Sat., Sun., public holidays 10am–6pm; Apr.–Sep.: Mon., Wed.–Sun. 10am–6pm* ● F25 🏛 🖼

Between 1830 and 1870, this former woodcutters' village in the forest of Fontainebleau became the favorite haunt of the landscape painters of the Barbizon School (Millet, Rousseau, Daubigny, Corot, Courbet). They stayed in the Auberge Ganne, which was converted into a municipal museum in 1995 and today holds temporary exhibitions. Its doors, walls and sideboards are still covered in paintings by anonymous artists. The house and studio of Jean-François Rousseau (55 Grande-Rue) is open to the public.

Musée national du château de Fontainebleau (13)
Château de Fontainebleau, 77300 Fontainebleau ☎ 01 60 71 50 70

🔲 ⊙ *June, Sep.–Oct.: Wed.–Mon. 9.30am–5pm; July–Aug. Wed.–Mon. 9.30am–6pm; Nov.–May: Wed.–Mon. 9.30am–12.30pm, 2–5pm; closed public holidays* ● *Parc free* **Grands Appartements, Musée chinois** F35; 18–25s F23; under-18s free 🖼 **Musée Napoléon Ier, Petits Appartements** F16 each; 18–25s F12 each; under-18s free 🏛

A royal residence since the Middle Ages, the chateau became a Renaissance palace (1527) during the reign of François I. It was Napoleon I's favorite residence and it was here that he took leave of his army in 1814. The palace, now a national museum, has retained both influences: Renaissance in the Galerie François Ier, and Empire in the Musée Napoléon. The gardens were designed by Le Nôtre. A glorious day out.

Not forgetting

▬ **Le Grand Veneur (E)** 77630 Barbizon ☎ 01 60 66 40 44 *Gastronomic cuisine* ●●●● ▬ **Croquembouche (F)** 43 rue France, 77300 Fontainebleau ☎ 01 64 22 01 57 *Traditional French cuisine* ●● ▬ **Auberge de Crisenoy (G)** Grande-Rue, 77390 Crisenoy ☎ 01 64 38 83 06 *Traditional French cuisine* ●●●

chateaux represented the aspirations of high-ranking officials (such as Vaux-le-Vicomte built by Louis XIV's finance minister).

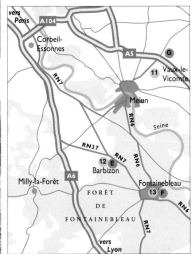

13

13

12

The doors and walls of the Auberge Ganne are decorated with frescoes, paintings and *trompe-l'oeil* effects.

12

11

13

Basic facts

Since the 1970s vast leisure areas and theme parks have been developed in the Paris region. Today, people come from all over the world to visit its three theme parks (among the largest in Europe) and 50 golf courses (10% of the golf courses in France).

► Further afield

Disneyland Paris (14)
77777 Marne-la-Vallée ☎ 01 64 74 30 00

■ ⊙ *Mon.–Fri. 10am–6pm; Sat., Sun. 9am–8pm ● 6 Jan.–Mar., Nov.–Dec. 20 F150; 3–11s F120; under-3s free; Mar.–Oct., Dec. 21–Jan. 5 F195; 3–11s F150; under-3s free* ⛨ ▣ ▦ *hotels, golf courses*

Disneyland Paris re-creates the magical world of Walt Disney, in five fantasy landscapes. A golden opportunity to meet heroes from children's books, legendary figures from the American Wild West and favorite Walt Disney characters. Attractions – and distractions – for all ages include Star Tour (a space voyage), the castle of Sleeping Beauty and golf courses.

15

Château de Thoiry and park (15)
78770 Thoiry-en-Yvelines ☎ 01 34 87 52 25

■ ⊙ *African game reserve Apr.–Sep.: Mon.–Sat. 10am–6pm; Sun., public holidays 10am–6.30pm; Oct.–Mar.: Mon.–Sat. 10am–5pm; Sun., public holidays 10am–6.30pm ● F100; 3–12s F79* ⊙ *Chateau Mon.–Fri. 2–5pm; Sat.–Sun. 2–6pm ● F30; 3–12s F25* ▣ ▦

The chateau (1564) was built by Philibert de l'Orme according to the 'golden section' principle. It creates a bridge of light through which the sun rises and sets on the days of the summer and winter solstices – a truly unique spectacle. The park is divided into French and English gardens, and a wildlife park that is home to some 800 animals. Visitors can drive through the 'African game reserve' and see the animals at close quarters, with the added protection of a double security fence for the lions and tigers. Don't miss the breathtaking aerial acrobatics of the birds of prey.

16

17

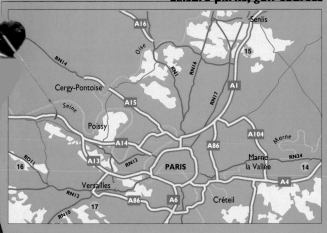

14

Parc Astérix (16)
BP 8 60128 Plailly ☎ 03 44 62 31 31

🕐 Apr.–July 15: Mon.–Fri. 10am–6pm; Sat., Sun. 9.30am–7pm / July 15–August: daily 9.30am–7pm; Sep.–Oct. 15: Wed. 10am–6pm, Sat., Sun. 9.30am–7pm ● F160, 3–11s F110, under-3s free, season tickets F320, 3–12s F22 ▣ 🏕 🖻 🏢

The park is based around Asterix the Gaul, the 'invincible' cartoon character created by Uderzo and Goscinny. Meet Asterix and his friends in their village. The park's other attractions include *rue de Paris* (Paris street), which traces the city's history, the Descente du Styx – a trip in a rubber dinghy on the underworld river of Greek mythology – and the Dolphinarium, with regular dolphin displays.

Golf national (17)
2 av. du Golf, 78280 Guyancourt ☎ 01 30 43 36 00
➡ 01 30 43 85 58

🕐 *Albatros* PAR 72, *Aigle* PAR 71, *Oiselet* PAR 32 daily 8am–7pm ● Mon.–Fri. F100–F220; Sat., Sun. F100–F330 ▣ 🏕 Côté Jardin ●● 🍸 Le Fairplay 🏌 🏢 Pro-shop

14

This showcase of the French Golf Federation has three courses: the 9-hole Oiselet (Birdie), the Aigle (Eagle), an 18-hole links-style course, and the Albatros (Albatross), ranked fourth in Europe, and the venue for the French Open, held every June. Stepping onto the Albatros is like stepping into another world, with a definite feel of Ireland about it. It is certainly an ideal course for improving your score! The friendly and professional welcome is 'on a par' with the quality of the courses.

Calling all bargain hunters

Designer seconds, ends of lines, factory stocks and second-hand items:

Le Mouton à cinq pattes *19 rue Grégoire-de-Tours, 75006* ☎ *01 43 29 73 56*

Réciproque *89, 92, 97, 101, 123 rue de la Pompe, 75016* ☎ *01 47 04 82 24*

Les Stocks de la rue d'Alésia *64–122 rue d'Alésia, 75016*

Where to shop

Tax refund

If you spend F2000 in one of the major department stores or in a store displaying the *Tax-Free Shopping* or *Cashback* logo, you can claim a VAT refund of around 14%. Make sure you take your passport.

Sales

The main sales periods are early February and July–August.

Salerooms

The largest auction house in Paris (buy a catalogue at newspaper kiosks) is the **Hôtel Richelieu-Drouot** *9 rue Drouot, 75009* ☎ *01 48 00 20 20*

On rainy days

Carrousel du Louvre *rue de Rivoli, 75001* A gallery of shops beneath the glass pyramid of the Louvre: Boutique des Musées de Paris, Virgin Megastore.
Galerie Véro-Dodat *19 rue Jean-Jacques-Rousseau, 75001* Includes, among others, Capia: a wonderful shop that sells old-fashioned dolls.
Galerie Vivienne *4 rue des Petits-Champs / 6 rue Vivienne, 75002* Original workshops and *salons de thé* in a period (1823) setting.

78
Shops
THE INSIDER'S FAVORITES

Basic facts

As well as being an integral part of everyday life in Paris, the city's huge, 19th-century department stores are also part of its cultural heritage. Life just wouldn't be the same without their back-to-school promotions, their wonderful Christmas window displays, their spring weddings lists or their

Where to shop

Le Bon Marché Rive Gauche (1)
22 rue de Sèvres, 75007 ☎ 01 44 39 80 00 ➡ 01 44 39 80 50

Ⓜ *Sèvres-Babylone* 🕐 *Mon.–Sat. 9.30am–7pm* 🔆 *La Grande Épicerie Mon.–Sat. 8.30am–9pm* ⬜ *Duty free for export, Reception desk*

Le Bon Marché offers its customers an international food department, an antiques gallery and a reading area furnished with easy chairs. The atmosphere is intimate and the emphasis is on old-fashioned personal service.

La Samaritaine (2)
19 rue de la Monnaie, 75001 ☎ 01 40 41 20 20 ➡ 01 40 41 28 28

Ⓜ *Pont-Neuf* 🕐 *Mon.–Wed., Fri.–Sat. 9.30am–7pm; Thur. 9.30am–10pm* ⬜ ⛩ *Le Toupary* ➡ *48* Ⓨ

A store with a popular appeal and a long-standing reputation for its particularly good DIY department. In 1996, it opted for a more stylish image when it opened its Grande Parfumerie, offering 40,000 leading beauty products, including perfumes and cosmetics, and giving over space to in-house beauty parlors by some of the top names. La Samaritaine's restaurant, Le Toupary, has a superb panoramic view of the city.

Les Galeries Lafayette (3)
40 boulevard Haussmann, 75009 ☎ 01 42 82 34 56 ➡ 01 48 78 25 19

Ⓜ *Havre-Caumartin, Opéra* 🕐 *Mon.–Wed., Fri.–Sat. 9.30am–7pm; Thur. 9.30am–9pm* ⬜ *Duty-free for export, Customer service desk* ⛩ Ⓓ

Les Galeries Lafayette offer a truly amazing range of services: easy shopping, while-you-wait heel bar, made-to-measure suits, hairdressing salons, travel agencies, booking agencies, as well as seven restaurants and a sushi bar. There are also regular in-store events such as fashion shows and concerts. On the home front: an entire story is given over to home decoration, with an area specially reserved for exclusive ideas by leading interior designers.

Le Printemps (4)
64 boulevard Haussmann, 75009 ☎ 01 42 82 50 00 ➡ 01 42 82 61 22

Ⓜ *Chaussée-d'Antin, Opéra* 🕐 *Mon.–Wed., Fri.–Sat. 9.35am–7pm; Thur. 9.35am–10pm* ⬜ *Duty-free for export, Priority desk* ⛩ *Brasserie Flo* 🔆

The 19th-century architecture and famous dome of this listed building are worth a visit in their own right. Here 9500 sq yds are devoted to women's fashion and another 18,000 sq yds to accessories. Decor simplified to the extreme enables customers to identify with themes and lifestyles without being distracted by over-elaborate surroundings.

Not forgetting

■ **FNAC (Fédération nationale d'achat des cadres) (5)**
26 avenue des Ternes, 75017 ☎ 01 44 09 18 00 *Active since 1954. This popular store sells books and records, as well as photographic, hi-fi and computer equipment, in permanent defiance of its rivals.*

big summer sales. Five major stores compete to offer the very best in brand names and labels, special presentations and events, and customer services.

DU PRINTEMPS

Elegant and expensive, the avenue Montaigne is the showcase for every kind of luxury and every kind of extravagance by the city's grand couturiers. All the top names are there. ■ Where to stay ➡ 22 ■ Where to eat ➡ 48 ■ After dark ➡ 92 ➡ 96

➡ Where to shop

Inès de la Fressange (6)
14 avenue Montaigne, 75008 ☎ 01 47 23 08 94 ➡ 01 47 23 05 54

M *Alma-Marceau, Franklin-Roosevelt* **Women's off-the-peg fashion, home decor** 🕒 *Mon.–Sat. 10am–6.30pm* ☐ *Duty-free for export, purchases mailed abroad*

A delightful designer boutique belonging to ex-Chanel supermodel Inès de la Fressange. Choose from a range of attractive personal items and decorative objects for the home in natural materials and 'healthy' colors. Take time out to try something on in the padded, boudoir-size cubicles.

Christian Lacroix (7)
26 avenue Montaigne, 75008 ☎ 01 47 20 68 95 ➡ 01 42 68 00 12

M *Alma-Marceau, Franklin-Roosevelt* **Haute couture, women's off-the-peg fashion** 🕒 *Mon.–Sat. 10am–7pm* ☐ *Duty-free for export, purchases mailed abroad*

While Lacroix's haute couture is the embodiment of beauty and elegance, the boutique's off-the-peg ranges are inspired by the warmth, color and baroque sentimentality of the designer's Provençal origins.

Christian Dior (8)
30 avenue Montaigne, 75008 ☎ 01 40 73 54 44 ➡ 01 47 20 00 60

M *Alma-Marceau, Franklin-Roosevelt* **Haute couture, women's and children's off-the-peg fashion, perfume, home decor** 🕒 *Tues.–Fri. 9.30am–6.30pm; Mon., Sat. 10am–6.30pm* ☐ *Duty-free for export* **¡¡** *Dior Homme 11 rue François-1ᵉʳ ☎ 01 40 73 54 46*

In this building Christian Dior launched the historic 'new look'. Dior's latest innovation is *Lady Dior*, a shopping bag whose topstitched canework motif is reminiscent of the Louis XV chairs on which customers used to sit when viewing collections. Such is its success that it is available in three sizes, seven different materials and five colors.

Nina Ricci (9)
39 avenue Montaigne, 75008 ☎ 01 49 52 57 31 ➡ 01 49 59 59

M *Alma-Marceau, Franklin-Roosevelt* **Haute couture, accessories, perfume** 🕒 *Mon.–Fri. 10am–6.30pm; Sat. 10am–1pm, 2.15–6.30pm* ☐ *Duty-free for export, purchases mailed abroad* **¡¡** *Ricci Prêt-à-porter 17 rue François-1ᵉʳ; Ricci Homme ➡ 144*

Nina Ricci has been given a more youthful look by Gilles Fuchs, who has introduced a breath of – resolutely modern – fresh air. The beauty products owe their rosy freshness to designers Garouste and Bonetti. The Lalique crystal bottles of *Air du Temps* are now available in a range of colors.

Not forgetting

■ **Joseph (10)** 14 av. Montaigne, 75008 ☎ 01 47 20 39 55 *Women's off-the-peg-fashion.* ■ **Vuitton (11)** 26 av. Montaigne, 75008 ☎ 01 45 62 47 00 *Accessories.* ■ **Caron (12)** 34 av. Montaigne, 75008 ☎ 01 47 23 40 82 *Perfume.* ■ **Mugler (13)** 49 av. Montaigne, 75008 ☎ 01 47 23 37 62 *Off-the-peg-fashion.*

This is a district of luxury hotels, radio stations, restaurants, theaters and movie theaters. In spite of the presence of the prestigious houses of Courrèges, Balmain and Rochas, the so-called 'golden triangle' is a predominately male preserve. The air is thick with tweed and resounds

Where to shop

Victoire Homme (14)
38 rue François-Ier, 75008 ☎ 01 47 23 89 81

 George-V **Off-the-peg menswear** 🕐 Tue.–Sat. 11am–2pm, 3–7pm ▬ ⬛
Victoire Femme ➡ 154

Exclusive collections of menswear aimed at the dashing forty-somethings who favor parkas, tweed suits and cashmere socks. A complete wardrobe, from shirts to swimming trunks, that has a slightly English flavor but is resolutely French in style.

Guerlain (15)
68 avenue des Champs-Élysées, 75008
☎ 01 45 62 52 57 ➡ 01 40 74 09 91

 Franklin-Roosevelt **Perfume** 🕐 Mon.–Sat. 10am–7pm ▬ Duty-free for export

In a decor that reflects the early 20th-century luxury of the most beautiful avenue in the world, Guerlain displays its magnificent perfumes (*Shalimar, L'Heure Bleue, Veytiver, Habit Rouge*) and eaux de toilette (*Impériale, Eau du coq, Eau de verveine*) like national treasures. They represent 150 years of perfumed seduction in all its forms: oils, essences, talcs, soaps, pot-pourri and candles.

La Maison du Chocolat (16)
56 rue Pierre-Charron, 75008 ☎ 01 47 23 38 25 ➡ 01 40 70 01 63

 Franklin-Roosevelt **Confectionery** 🕐 Mon.–Sat. 9.30am–7pm ▬

A vice becomes a virtue in the 'house of chocolate', where addicts can unashamedly enjoy the delights of creamy hot chocolate made with bitter chocolate, and laced with rum or flavored with spices. The confectionery range includes 30 varieties of dark-chocolate ganache (flavored with jasmine, basil, rosemary, bush peach, cherry plums) and champagne truffles.

Faguais (17)
30 rue de la Trémoille, 75008 ☎ 01 47 20 80 91

 Alma-Marceau, Franklin-Roosevelt **Delicatessen** 🕐 Mon.–Sat. 9.15am–7.30pm ▬

French regional specialties feature prominently among the distinctive flavors of this traditional delicatessen. Its range of some 2000 traditionally made products conjures up Proustian images of nougat from Montélimar, dark red plums from Agen and *calissons* (diamond-shaped, almond-flavored sweets) from Aix-en-Provence. House classics include the *mélange Faguais* (a blend of teas from India, China and Sri Lanka), a jam made with three different citrus fruits, and such 'limited editions' as its pasteurized pickles which have to be ordered in advance!

■ **Ricci Club Hommes (18)** 19 rue François-Ier, 75008 ☎ 01 49 52 57 39 *Off-the-peg menswear, accessories* ■ **Weston (19)** 114 avenue des Champs-Élysées, 75008 ☎ 01 45 62 26 47 *Men's and women's footwear* ■ **Cartier (20)** 51 rue François-Ier, 75008 ☎ 01 40 74 61 83 *Jewelry, perfume.*

to the trilling of mobile
phones. ■ Where to stay ➔
22 ■ Where to eat ➔ 66 ➔
74 ■ After dark ➔ 86 ➔ 96.

In the area

Faubourg Saint-Honoré, bounded by the Palais de l'Élysée, rue Royale and place de la Concorde, has a number of stylish 'historic monuments'. The world-famous and truly unique studio-fashion houses of Hermès, Lanvin, Laroche and Au Nain Bleu combine tradition and expertise with a witty,

Where to shop

Hermès (21)
24 rue du Faubourg Saint-Honoré, 75008 ☎ 01 40 17 47 17

Ⓜ Concorde **Accessories, perfume** 🕓 Mon.–Sat. 10am–6.30pm
⬛ Duty-free for export

The famous Hermès scarves and animal motif ties still sell like hot cakes. However, the house specialty remains its saddle-stitched leather, made in the Hermès workshops. Other popular items include bags (Bugatti, Kelly) and even shoe-trees and mobile-phone cases.

Au Nain Bleu (22)
406–410 rue Saint-Honoré, 75008 ☎ 01 42 60 39 01 ➡ 01 42 61 75 67

Ⓜ Concorde **Toys** 🕓 Mon.–Sat. 9.45am–6.30pm ⬛ Duty-free for export, purchases mailed abroad

The oldest toyshop in Paris remains young at heart and continues to delight young and old alike with its remarkable window displays. From handmade wooden blocks to electric Ferraris, its toys have evolved over the years to keep pace with changing fashions.

Lanvin Hommes (23)
15 rue du Faubourg Saint-Honoré, 75008 ☎ 01 44 71 31 33

Ⓜ Concorde **Off-the-peg menswear** 🕓 Mon.–Sat 10am–6.45pm ⬛ 🍴 Café Bleu 🔼 **Lanvin Femme** 22 rue du Faubourg Saint-Honoré ☎ 01 44 71 31 73

Jeanne Lanvin has impressed her style on the very walls (decorated by sculptor Albert Rateau) of her fashion houses, where the degree of luxury is directly related to the floor level. From the first-story leisurewear, casuals and accessories, you move up through off-the-peg fashions. By the time you reach the sixth story, made-to-measure suits are made for a clientele who each have a personal dossier of precisely recorded details so that they can place an order from anywhere in the world. Distinctive panamas by Gelot sit alongside more ordinary hats, while the tie collection runs into the hundreds.

Lalique (24)
11 rue Royale, 75008 ☎ 01 53 05 12 12 ➡ 01 42 65 59 06

Ⓜ Concorde, Madeleine **Home decor** 🕓 Mon.–Sat. 9.30am–6.30pm
⬛ Duty-free for export

Lalique crystal at its dazzling best: classic vases, champagne goblets and flutes. The boutique has been extended to include accessories, from handbags and belts with crystal clasps to colored pendants and Lalique translucent rings.

Not forgetting

⬛ **Ladurée (25)** 16 rue Royale, 75001 ☎ 01 42 60 21 79 *Patisserie*
⬛ **Jadis et Gourmande (26)** 27 rue Boissy-d'Anglas, 75008 ☎ 01 42 65 23 23 *Confectionery.* ⬛ **Guy Laroche (27)** 28–30 rue du Fbg Saint-Honoré, 75008 ☎ 01 42 65 62 74 *Haute couture, women's off-the-peg fashion.* ⬛ **Loft (28)** 12 rue du Fbg St-Honoré, 75008 ☎ 01 42 65 59 65 *Women's off-the-peg fashion.*

modern elegance. ■ Where to stay ➡ 22 ■ Where to eat ➡ 62 ➡ 66

23

21

27

21

26

24

Scooters (from F435) are among the many traditional toys offered by Au Nain Bleu.

22

The district is dominated by the vast 19th-century church of La Madeleine, intended to echo the Parthenon in Athens. Like the church, the district has more presence than actual charm. However, it does have a remarkable vitality, as well as a number of magnificent shops (mostly

Where to shop

Gien (29)
18 rue de l'Arcade, 75008 ☎ 01 42 66 52 32 ➡ 01 42 65 15 77

M Madeleine, Havre-Caumartin **Home decor** ◷ Tue.–Sat. 10am–7pm ▣ Duty-free for export, purchases mailed abroad

A huge wall display presents the dozens of different styles of plate blazoned in blue and white for which Gien has been famous for almost 200 years. On the second floor, tables are set with traditional and modern-style dinner services. A collection of teapots decorated with country motifs adds a touch of rural charm.

Paraboot (30)
13 rue Vignon, 75008 ☎ 01 47 42 55 05 ➡ 01 47 42 55 08

M Madeleine **Men's, women's and children's footwear** ◷ Mon.–Sat. 10am–7pm ▣ Duty-free for export ⑪ 9 rue de Grenelle, 75007 ☎ 01 45 49 24 26

Paraboot is renowned for its leisure-sports footwear and for ensuring that the Paris sporting set, from hikers to horse riders, is well-shod. The leather is hand cut from traditionally tanned, top-quality skins, while rubber soles ensure flexibility and durability. If you don't hunt, shoot or fish, Paraboot also offers some superb moccasins and lace-ups.

Hédiard (31)
21 place de la Madeleine, 75008 ☎ 01 43 12 88 88 ➡ 01 42 66 31 97

M Madeleine **Delicatessen** ◷ Mon.–Sat. 9am–9pm **Caterer** ◷ Mon.–Sat. 9am–11pm ▣ Purchases mailed abroad ⑪⑪ Mon.–Sat. 9am–11pm

Hédiard makes ordinary food look like decorative art, with its rows of colored jams, mustards and other preserves. Fruits for all seasons, from all over the world, are arranged in still lifes that would do credit to Giuseppe Arcimboldo (1530–93). Here, lovers of fine foods find that their vice becomes an esthetic pleasure to be indulged unrestrainedly. Hédiard also offers an unlimited choice of wines and champagnes.

Peter (32)
33 rue Boissy-d'Anglas, 75008 ☎ 01 40 07 05 38 ➡ 01 40 07 05 35

M Madeleine, Concorde **Goldsmiths and silversmiths** ◷ Mon.–Sat 9.30am–6.30pm ▣ Duty-free for export

Renowned for tableware that graces the most sumptuous tables, and cutlery that combines vermilion and solid silver with ebony, ivory, jade, onyx and other precious materials. Part of the work is always carried out on the premises. In recent years, ranges have become more accessible and now include versions which are dishwasher-proof and attractively priced (ideal for wedding lists!) while losing none of their prestige.

Not forgetting
■ **Blanc Bleu (33)** 5 boulevard de la Madeleine, 75008 ☎ 01 47 42 02 18 Sportswear. ■ **Pierre Frey (34)** 22 rue Royale, 75008 ☎ 01 49 26 04 77 A range of magnificent furnishing fabrics.

devoted to home decor and gastronomic pleasures) in a relatively small area. ■ Where to stay ➡ 26 ■ Where to eat ➡ 62

32

30

29

La Madeleine, where exquisite flavors and sophisticated tableware go hand in hand.

31

32

Where to shop

Liste Rouge (35)
25 place Vendôme, 75001 ☎ 01 42 60 32 95 ➠ 01 42 61 53 29

Ⓜ Tuileries, Opéra **Men's and women's shirts and blouses** 🕐 (by appointment) Tue.–Sat. 10am–1pm, 2–6.30pm ▣ Duty-free for export, purchases mailed abroad

Perfectly finished made-to-measure shirts and blouses, with hand-embroidered monograms and Australian mother-of-pearl buttons, at surprisingly reasonable prices. The only problem experienced by its 10,000 customers who place regular mail orders is which of its 1000 fabrics to choose.

Philippe Model (36)
33 place du Marché Saint-Honoré, 75001 ☎ 01 42 96 89 02

Ⓜ Tuileries, Opéra **Hats, men's and women's footwear** 🕐 Tue.–Fri. 10am–7pm; Sat.1–7pm ▣ Duty-free for export

The season's creative designs are premiered at the spring race meetings, especially the *Prix de Diane-Hermès* at Chantilly, where the extravagant hats are on show. Designs for everyday wear are up-to-the-minute but more restrained.

Maria Luisa (37)
2 rue Cambon, 75001 ☎ 01 47 03 96 15 ➠ 01 47 03 94 17

Ⓜ Concorde **Women's off-the-peg fashion** 🕐 Mon.–Sat. 10.30am–7pm ▣ Duty-free for export

This young Venezuelan uses personal taste and intuition to choose the very best of the very latest in French fashion design. Ranges include designs by Eric Bergère – elegant, simple and witty.

Meyrowitz (38)
5 rue de Castiglione, 75001 ☎ 01 42 60 63 64 ➠ 01 42 61 36 30

Ⓜ Tuileries **Opticians, optical instruments** 🕐 Mon.–Sat. 9.30–6pm ▣ Duty-free for export

Alfonso XIII of Spain, Edward VIII of England and the Aga Khan are just three of the prestigious 'regulars' whose favorite styles are now available in exclusive gold and tortoiseshell designs. In the 1930s Meyrowitz produced the goggles worn by early aviators. Today, it offers a range of binoculars, barometers and prescription spectacles.

Not forgetting
■ **Dinh Van (39)** 18 rue de la Paix, 75002 ☎ 01 42 61 74 49 *Jewelry, accessories.* ■ **Poiray (40)** 8 rue de la Paix, 75002 ☎ 01 42 61 70 58 *Jewelry.* ■ **Daum (41)** 4 rue de la Paix, 75002 ☎ 01 42 61 25 25 *Home decor.* ■ **Charvet (42)** 28 place Vendôme, 75001 ☎ 01 42 60 30 70 *Men's made-to measure shirts.* ■ **Chanel (43)** 31 rue Cambon, 75001 ☎ 01 42 86 28 00 *Haute couture, off-the-peg fashion, perfume.* ■ **Bob Shop (44)** 20 rue Cambon, 75001 ☎ 01 40 15 96 55 *Women's trousers.* ■ **Longchamp (45)** 390 rue Saint-Honoré, 75001 ☎ 01 42 60 00 00 *Accessories.*

Place Vendôme E A-B2

eat ➡ 62 ➡ 64 ➡ 74
■ After dark ➡ 88 ➡ 90
■ What to see ➡ 104

R. Scribe
M Opéra
44
45
Bd des Capucines
Rue de la Paix
Avenue de l'Opéra
12
17
Rue
Daunou
31
40
39
41
R. des Capucines
R. D. Casanova
R. Gomboust
32
42
35
PLACE
Place du
Marché
St-Honoré
36
43
30
29
VENDÔME
39
44
37
Rue
Saint-
Honoré
40
45
Rue de Castiglione
19
20
38
Rue du Mt - Thabor
41
21
37
22
Rue de
Rivoli
M
47
Tuileries
M
3
Concorde
JARDIN DES
TUILERIES
36

37

39

37

43

43

CHANEL
PARFUM
N°5
CHANEL
PARIS

43

151

In the area

Until the 17th century, the Palais-Royal was the Paris residence of the kings of France. For a long time after that, it remained the exclusive venue of the capital's most elegant women, and a secret garden visited by writers and children. Today, priceless treasures are concealed beneath its arcades.

Where to shop

Legrand (46)
1 rue de la Banque, 75002 ☎ 01 42 60 07 12 ➡ 01 42 61 25 51

M *Palais-Royal* **Delicatessen, wine cellar** 🕐 *Tue.–Fri. 8.30am–7.30pm; Sat. 8.30am–1pm, 3–7pm* ✉ *Purchases mailed abroad*

A must for connoisseurs of regional wines, fine alcohols and chocolates. Ranges include the famous *Ébène* (70% cocoa) from Weiss, makers of chocolate in Saint-Étienne since 1882, and all kinds of great and lesser vintages selected by the second generation of the Legrand family. They have also had the good taste to retain the original storage jars and decor of this traditional grocer's store near the Paris Stock Exchange.

Maison de Vacances (47)
63–64 galerie Montpensier, 75001 ☎ 01 47 03 99 74 ➡ 01 47 03 99 24

M *Palais-Royal* **Home decor** 🕐 *Mon. 1–7pm; Tue.–Fri. 11am–7pm* ✉ *Duty-free for export, purchases mailed abroad*

Michèle Foulks bases her 'chamber music' theme on three complementary tones – cream, ecru and celadon – and a perfect contrast of soft and rough textures. Sheets, blankets and pajamas in loosely woven, unbleached linen, cashmere or angora. All items can be individually monogrammed, from the photo album in its linen case to the breakfast set for two in white and gold porcelain, from the table linen to the toweling and lawn bathroom linen.

Les Salons du Palais-Royal Shiseido (48)
142 galerie de Valois, 75001 ☎ 01 49 27 09 09 ➡ 01 49 27 92 12

M *Palais-Royal* **Perfume, cosmetics** 🕐 *Mon.–Sat. 9am–7pm* ✉ *Duty-free for export*

A showcase for the perfumes created by Serge Lutens for Shiseido. An experience to delight the senses, from the apothecary's bottles displaying brightly-colored contents – *Iris* (pale mauve), *Fleur d'Oranger* (mandarin), *Myrthe* (bright red), *Ambre* (cognac colored) and *Rose de Nuit* (lemon) – to the veritable symphony of scents. The experience is completed by deliciously fragrant green tea served while your purchases are being expertly and exquisitely gift-wrapped.

Didier Ludot (49)
24 galerie Montpensier, 75001 ☎ 01 42 96 06 56

M *Palais-Royal* **Antiques, haute couture** 🕐 *Mon.–Sat. 10.30am–7pm* ✉

Second-hand clothes, shoes, handbags and luggage by Chanel, Hermès, Balenciaga, Ciurrèges, Balmain, Givenchy, Dior and Vuitton. A collector's boutique that could compete with the fashion museum ➡ 106. A must for devotees of Dior's 'little black dress'.

Not forgetting

■ **Castelbajac (50)** 5 rue des Petits-Champs, 75002 ☎ 01 42 60 37 33 *Off-the-peg menswear, women's and children's fashion and accessories in noble materials and bright colors.*

■ Where to eat ➡ 70 ■ After dark
➡ 90 ■ What to see ➡ 104 ➡ 106

46

48

48

50

47

50

The place des Victoires provides a link between what was once the intellectual center of Paris (Palais-Royal) and the so-called *ventre de Paris* (belly of Paris), Les Halles food market before it was transferred to Rungis. In the wake of such pioneers as Kenzo and Victoire, established

Where to shop

Bonpoint (51)
50 rue Étienne-Marcel, 75001 ☎ 01 40 26 20 90

Ⓜ *Les Halles* **Children's off-the-peg fashion, home decor** 🕐 *Mon.–Sat. 10am–7pm* ▣ *Duty free for export* 🔀 *67 rue de l'Université, 75007* ☎ *01 45 55 63 70*

A paradise for spoiled children and their parents. Smocked dresses, patent-leather shoes, furniture and a range of beautifully selected gifts for new arrivals. Bonpoint also offers a range of dresses and practical wear for mothers-to-be.

Ventilo (52)
27bis rue du Louvre, 75001 ☎ 01 42 33 18 67 ➡ 01 44 76 83 02

Ⓜ *Les Halles* **Women's off-the-peg fashion, home decor** 🕐 *Mon. noon–7pm; Tue.–Sat. 10.30am–7pm* ▣ 🕐 *Mon.–Sat. noon–5.30pm* ☎ *01 44 76 82 97* 🔀 *59, rue Bonaparte 75006* ☎ *01 43 26 64 84*

Three stories of casual and easy-to-wear summer and winter fashions in natural materials and fabrics, presented in a natural wood setting. The home decor department is on the top floor, next to the restaurant-*salon de thé*, a favorite meeting place for the journalists and fashion set of the place des Victoires.

Kenzo (53)
3 place des Victoires, 75001 ☎ 01 40 39 72 03 ➡ 01 40 39 72 05

Ⓜ *Les Halles* **Off-the-peg menswear and women's fashion** 🕐 *Mon. 11am–7pm; Tue.–Sat. 10am–7pm* ▣ *Duty free for export* 🔀 *16–17 boulevard Raspail 75007* ☎ *01 42 22 09 38*

Bright colors, unusual prints and beautiful tailoring by this most Parisian of Japanese fashion boutiques. Sophisticated fashions, dresses in lightweight fabrics and rich brocades for women; dark suits, shirts in every color and extravagant ties for men; and a reasonably priced 'Jungle' range for the younger generation.

Victoire Femme (54)
12 place des Victoires, 75001 ☎ 01 42 61 09 02 ➡ 01 47 03 99 12

Ⓜ *Les Halles* **Women's off-the-peg fashion** 🕐 *Mon.–Sat. 10am–7pm* ▣ *Duty free for export* 🔀 *I rue Madame, 75006* ☎ *01 45 44 28 14* ; *Victoire Homme* ➡ *144*

The latest designs and accessories for a clientele that, for the past 20 years, has become accustomed to the best in modern fashion. Next door, a sister boutique offers easy-to-wear fashion at affordable prices.

Not forgetting

■ **Piétrement Lambert et Cie (55)** 58 rue Jean-Jacques-Rousseau, 75001 ☎ 01 42 33 30 50 *Pâté de foie gras, game, capons, truffles.* ■ **Claudie Pierlot (56)** 4 rue du Jour, 75001 ☎ 01 42 21 38 38 *Women's off-the-peg fashion.* ■ **Agnès B. (57)** 2, 3, 6, 10, rue du Jour, 75001 ☎ 01 45 08 56 56 *Off-the-peg fashion for men, women and children, cosmetics, accessories.*

in the 1970s, other designers moved into and gradually transformed the district.
■ Where to eat ➡ 70

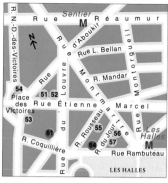

54

51

53

54

52

51

51

For a long time, Saint-Germain-des-Prés was a village combining provincial charm with intellectual sophistication. Today, fashion boutiques have replaced the old bookstores and shops selling objets d'art.
■ Where to stay ➡ 38 ➡ 40 ➡ 42 ■ Where to eat ➡ 78

Where to shop

Deyrolle (58)
46 rue du Bac, 75007 ☎ 01 42 22 30 07

Ⓜ *Rue-du-Bac* **Stuffed animals, natural science supplies, educational posters** ◐ *Mon.–Sat. 10am–1pm, 2–6.30pm* ▣

Established in 1831, Deyrolle is more like the Natural History Museum ➡ 120 than a shop that sells stuffed animals. An avid clientele of interior designers. One of the most extraordinary shops in Europe – well worth a look.

Debauve & Gallais (59)
30 rue des Saint-Pères, 75007 ☎ 01 45 48 54 67 ➡ 01 45 48 21 78

Ⓜ *Saint-Germain-des-Prés* **Confectionery** ◐ *Mon.–Sat. 9am–7pm* ▣ *Duty-free for export*

In the 18th century, this store supplied royalty with fine chocolate: double-vanilla flavored chocolate for the king and chocolate drops flavored with almond oil for the queen. It acquired a new dimension when a pharmacist extended the range with 'healthy' (sugar-free) chocolate and coffee-flavored chocolate for 'addicts'. Specialties include *Théobroma*, the world's darkest chocolate (99% cocoa), and *Grains d'Arabica*, coffee beans in dark chocolate.

L'Artisan Parfumeur (60)
24 boulevard Raspail, 75007 ☎ 01 42 22 23 32

Ⓜ *Rue-du-Bac, Sèvres-Babylone* **Perfume** ◐ *Mon.–Sat. 10.30am–7pm* ▣ *Duty-free for export*

'Alternative' perfumes, with variations on a theme (fig, mimosa, leaf), in subtly different blends for personal use or for use in the home. For example, Mikados are silk sachets that will give your cupboards and closets the evocative scent of old polished wood wardrobes.

Arnys (61)
14 rue de Sèvres, 75007 ☎ 01 45 48 76 99 ➡ 01 45 48 84 72

Ⓜ *Sèvres-Babylone* **Off-the-peg menswear** ◐ *Mon. 10am–1pm, 2–7pm; Tue.–Sat. 10am–7.30pm* ▣ *Duty-free for export, purchases mailed abroad*

The quintessence of Rive-Gauche fashion encapsulated in a range of traditional styles 'revisited': from the corded-velvet lumber jacket with its colored wool lining to the high-waisted trousers with suspenders (as worn by the Duke of Windsor) that conceal the stomach. Each new suit is made to measure before being brought out in an off-the-peg version. Shirts have 26 different styles of collar and 7 different styles of cuff.

Not forgetting
■ **Corinne Zaquine (62)** 38 rue de Grenelle, 75007 ☎ 01 45 48 93 03 *Women's hats.* ■ **Rodika Zanian (63)** 8 rue de la Chaise, 75007 ☎ 01 45 49 25 73 *Women's off-the-peg fashion.* ■ **Martine Sitbon (64)** 13 rue de Grenelle, 75007 ☎ 01 44 39 84 44 *Women's off-the-peg fashion.* ■ **C.F.O.C. (65)** 163 bvd Saint-Germain, 75006 ☎ 01 45 48 00 18 *Home decor.*

■ After dark
➡ 86 ➡ 88
➡ 98 ■ What
to see ➡ 116

ARNYS

61

64

58

DEYROLLE

58

59

60

L'Artisan Parfumeur

Corinne Zaquine

62

64

Place Saint-Sulpice is only a stone's throw from the busy district of Saint-Germain-des-Prés. For a long time it was a peaceful oasis, bounded by the church and fountain of Saint-Sulpice, near the Jardin du Luxembourg ➡ 122. The 1980s saw the arrival of the first of the boutiques that today

➡ Where to shop

Erès (66)
4bis rue du Cherche-Midi, 75006 ☎ 01 45 44 95 54 ➡ 01 40 32 43 48

Ⓜ Saint-Sulpice **Women's swimwear** 🕐 Mon.–Sat. 10am–7pm ▣ Duty-free for export

Unrivaled for its beautiful swimwear. Every season sees around 100 new designs by Irène Leroux. Since 1965, she has continued to find new materials and colors while maintaining the athletic yet sophisticated elegance for which the label is renowned.

Poilâne (67)
8 rue du Cherche-Midi, 75006 ☎ 01 45 48 42 59 ➡ 01 45 44 99 80

Ⓜ Sèvres-Babylone **Bread, Viennese bread and patisserie** 🕐 Mon.–Sat. 7.15am–8.15pm ▣

The pictures hanging on the walls and a unique library trace Poilâne's history through three generations of bread-making. Today, Lionel Poilâne perpetuates the art of traditional bread-making, leaving his dough to rise in wicker baskets lined with linen. The shop is always full and, at certain times of the day, customers queue for brioches and apple tarts.

Delage (68)
6 rue Mézières, 75006 ☎ 01 42 84 15 24 ➡ 01 42 84 15 26

Ⓜ Saint-Sulpice **Women's footwear** 🕐 Mon., Sat. 10am–1pm, 2–6.45pm; Wed.–Fri. 10am–6.45pm ▣ Duty-free for export, purchases mailed abroad

Sheer luxury in the form of simply designed, leather footwear weighing only a few ounces and available in a wide range of unusual colors. Made from wild animal skins: crocodile (30 shades), ostrich, shagreen, lizard (60 shades) and sharkskin for court shoes, moccasins and boots of varying widths, styles and heel-heights. Routine repairs are carried out using the original last in the boutique's own workshops.

A.P.C. (69)
3–4 rue de Fleurus, 75006 ☎ 01 42 22 12 77 ➡ 01 45 44 75 22

Ⓜ Saint-Placide **Off-the-peg menswear and women's fashion** 🕐 Mon.–Sat. 10.30am–7pm ▣ Duty-free for export 🔟 **Surplus** 32 rue Cassette, 75006 ☎ 01 45 48 43 71; **General store** (accessories) 45 rue Madame, 75006 ☎ 01 45 48 72 42

In less than ten years, this label has achieved worldwide acclaim. Its success lies in its exclusive range of materials and colors, traditional expertise and the 'revolutionary normality' of a basic and extremely versatile wardrobe. Off-the-peg menswear and women's fashion have been extended by a range of accessories from two new nearby boutiques.

Not forgetting
■ **Robert Clergerie (70)** 5 rue du Cherche-Midi, 75006 ☎ 01 45 48 75 47 A must for women's footwear: elegant, fashionable and comfortable.

crowd the area, devoted to fashion and interiors. ■ Where to stay ➡ 42 ■ Where to eat ➡ 78 ➡ 82 ■ What to see ➡ 122 ■ What to buy ➡ 140

66

67

67

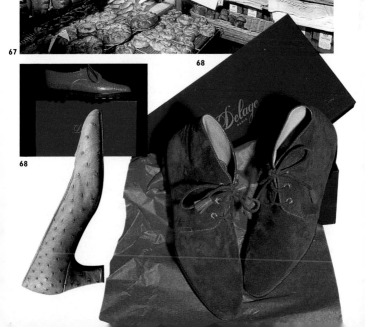

68

68

Apart from its sale rooms, Paris is full of art galleries, antiques galleries, second-hand stores, flea markets ➡ 162 and world famous craftsmen. They tend to be grouped in streets or blocks, forming 'little villages'. Parisians like nothing better than to go there to stroll or to look for

Where to shop

Le Village Suisse (71)
78 avenue de Suffren, 75015

Ⓜ *La Motte-Picquet-Grenelle Second-hand shops* Ⓢ *Thur.–Mon. 10.30am–7pm*

There is nothing remotely Swiss about this friendly 'village' near the Eiffel Tower, where local families take their Sunday stroll. Dozens of tiny shops offer an eclectic range of good-quality merchandise, from traditional English-style items, rustic furniture, and curios from Africa to light fittings and ornaments.

Carré Rive Gauche (72)
Rues des Saints-Pères, du Bac, de l'Université and quai Voltaire, 75007

Ⓜ *Rue-du-Bac* Ⓟ *Antiques, art galleries* Ⓢ *Mon.–Sat. 10am–6pm* ⊟

A host of art galleries and antiques shops have turned one of the oldest and quietest districts in Paris into a vast and fascinating showcase – furniture, paintings, porcelain and valuable carpets – that combines past and present. In May, the Carré holds a five-day event known as the 'Objet Extraordinaire' (unusual object). During this period, every window becomes a curiosity shop, and the district a regular Aladdin's cave as it turns the spotlight on its most extravagant and unusual pieces.

72

73

74

collectors' items, or both. As well as reflecting past and present cultures, these 'villages' are also excellent indicators of fashion.

Le Louvre des Antiquaires (73)
2 place du Palais-Royal, 75001
☎ 01 42 97 27 00

M *Palais-Royal* **P** *Antiques* 🕓 *Sep.– June: Tue.–Sun. 11am–7pm / July–Aug.: Tue.–Sat. 11am–7pm* ▣ *Expert advice by appointment*

The Louvre des Antiquaires is a vast three-story gallery that stands almost next door to the Louvre Museum ➡ 104. It houses some 250 top antique shops selling jewelry, paintings, tapestries and porcelain. Although this indoor gallery is warm and cozy in winter, the open-air markets are much more fun in summer.

Le Viaduc des Arts (74)
9–129 avenue Daumesnil, 75012 ☎ 01 43 45 98 98

M *Gare-de-Lyon* **P** *Traditional crafts* 🕓 *Mon.–Thur. 9am–1pm, 2–6pm; Fri. 9am–1pm, 2–5pm* ▣ 🍸 🏠 🖥

A disused railway viaduct has been converted into an impressive series of traditional craft workshops and galleries that stretch for a mile. Its arches house stonecutters, cabinet-makers, glass artists, embroiderers, feather dealers, calligraphers, costumiers, stringed-instrument makers, confectioners, artists and photographers, as well as restaurants and bistros. Along the top of the old viaduct, the tree-lined avenue of the 'Coulée verte' stretches from the Bastille to Reuilly.

Not forgetting

■ **Village Saint-Paul (75)** rues Saint-Paul and Charlemagne, 75004 *Antiques* 🕓 *Thur.–Mon. 10am–7pm*

73

72

73

Basic facts

The many second-hand shops and stalls of Saint-Ouen (76), the noisy flea markets (*marchés aux puces*) of Montreuil (77) and the charming pavement 'stalls' of Vanves (78) are full of idle onlookers, dedicated sightseers and buyers looking for bargains.

➤ Where to shop

Puces de Saint-Ouen

Ⓜ *Porte-de-Clignancourt*
Ⓢ *Sat.–Mon. 9.30am–7pm*

This world famous market is the oldest and largest of the Paris flea markets. It was established in the 19th century and today covers 8.6 acres, with 9 miles of aisles, 2,000 stalls and 150,000 visitors per week. The Saint-Ouen (or more precisely Clignancourt) flea market in fact consists of ten or so smaller markets, each defined by the quality, price and style of its merchandise.

Marché Vernaison

Ⓢ *Sat.–Mon.*
☎ *01 40 12 10 14*

Furniture and knick-knacks. The oldest and most charming of the Saint-Ouen flea markets. It was named after Romain Vernaison who used to rent his land to rag-and-bone merchants so they could sell china vases at the foot of the city's fortifications, where traders were exempt from the city toll. By 1920, the land was occupied by second-hand dealers. Édith Piaf made her debut at Chez Louisette, the bistro at aisle 10.

Marché Biron

Antiques and other items of value. Beautiful and well-restored, but expensive furniture.

Marché Malik

This is the 'in' place for hard-up trendies. Enter via rue Jules Vallès whose stalls are piled high with second-hand clothes, kitchen utensils and records.

Marché Malassis

A fine selection of antiques and furniture in a modern building.

Marché Dauphine

Contemporary art and old furniture displayed over two stories.

Marché Serpette

Stallholders here undertake to sell only old items. Goods on sale include quality leather armchairs, old-fashioned knick-knacks and beautiful wood furniture.

Marché Paul-Bert

Second-hand goods, pewter, bronze statues, porcelain, Chinese ornaments, ironware and other items that seem to have come straight out of people's attics: a truly uplifting experience!

Marché Jules-Vallès

Toys, crafts, accessories and rustic furniture.

DÉBUT DU MARCHÉ AUX PUCES

THE DICK TURPIN INN

SCÈNE DE MÉNAGE MAGASIN D'USI...

Puces de Montreuil

M *Porte-de-Montreuil*
⏰ *Sat.–Mon. 8am–6pm*

This noisy and popular flea market is situated on the Périphérique (Paris ring road). Although not the place to go if you want to enjoy a quiet stroll, it is the most amazing of the Paris flea markets. You have to fight your way past rolls of fabrics at F10 per meter (yard) piles of bicycles for under F900 each, batteries for every kind of vehicle, charming knick-knacks that once belonged to a set, piles of second-hand clothes…

Puces de Vanves

M *Porte-de-Vanves (avenue Georges-Lafenestre)*
⏰ *Sat.–Sun. 7am–7pm*

Smaller than Saint-Ouen and more civilized than Montreuil. The merchandise is laid at your feet… on the pavement. The antiques are neat and tidy, the knick-knacks charming and the wood furniture (although not always period) reasonable. It is advisable to get there early, as this is a small market and the bargains don't last long. For second-hand clothes and kitchen utensils, rue Marc Sangnier is a real bargain basement.

A word or two of advice…

● Travel to the markets by subway. It is impossible to park near the markets and incorrectly parked cars are soon towed away by the police.

● Don't be put off buying larger items of furniture. Stallholders will deliver within the Paris area when the market closes.

● Get there early so as not to miss the best bargains. Alternatively, it can sometimes be easier to negotiate a price at closing time.

● Bear in mind that stallholders do not willingly discuss business at lunchtime!

● Bargain by all means, but not indiscriminately. It is better to find a fault that enables you to reasonably offer a lower price rather than automatically asking for a 50% reduction.

● Make sure you take cash with you. It is easier to strike a bargain with cash, and there are always long queues at the cash machines.

● The Saint-Ouen and Montreuil flea markets are open on Mondays (only a few stalls are closed). It is easier to strike a deal on a Monday when the markets are less crowded and stallholders are more readily available.

FIN
DU MARCHÉ
AUX PUCES

Finding your way

Arrondissements
Paris has 20 *arrondissements* (districts), numbered in a spiral from the center (Ile de la Cité) outward. They correspond to the capital's historic boundaries.

10 Maps

Rive Droite and Rive Gauche

The River Seine divides Paris both geographically and culturally. The Rive Droite (Right Bank) is linked with business and commerce, while the Rive Gauche (Left Bank) is synonymous with culture. This division dates from the 12th century and reached its height in the 1930s, when Saint-Germain-des-Prés claimed to be the intellectual center of the world. Today the terms Rive Droite and Rive Gauche are still more closely associated with a particular lifestyle than a geographical location.

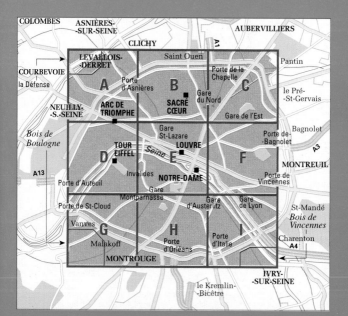

Street index

Each street name is followed by a bold letter indicating which map to refer to, and a grid reference.

Index

Abbreviations

Av. = avenue	m. = métro	pte = porte	sq. = square
bd = boulevard	pl. = place	r. = rue	

Métro map

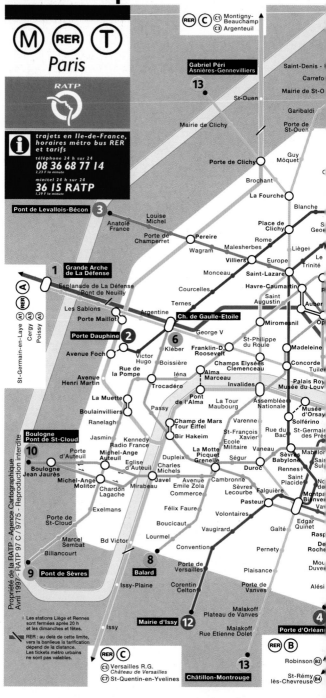

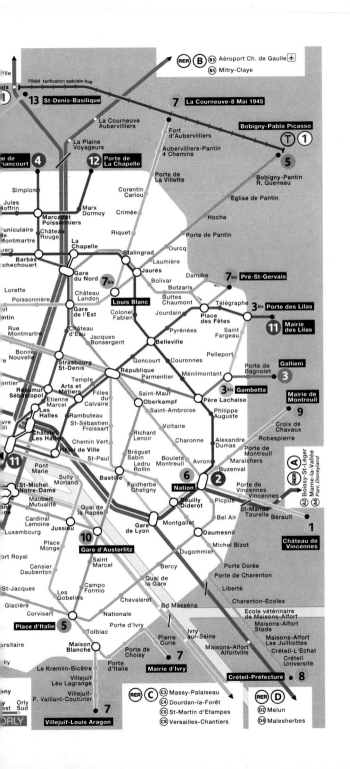

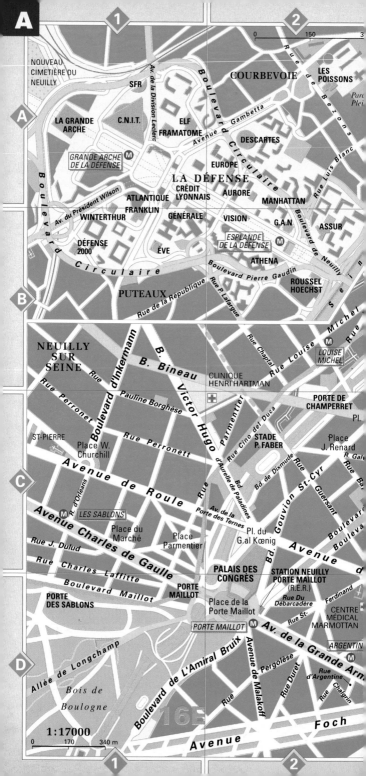

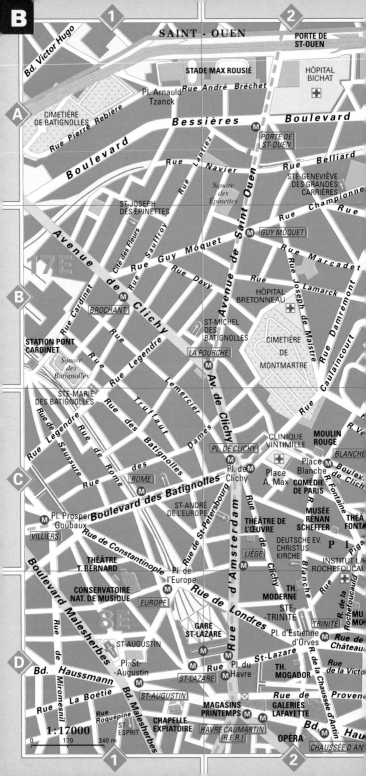

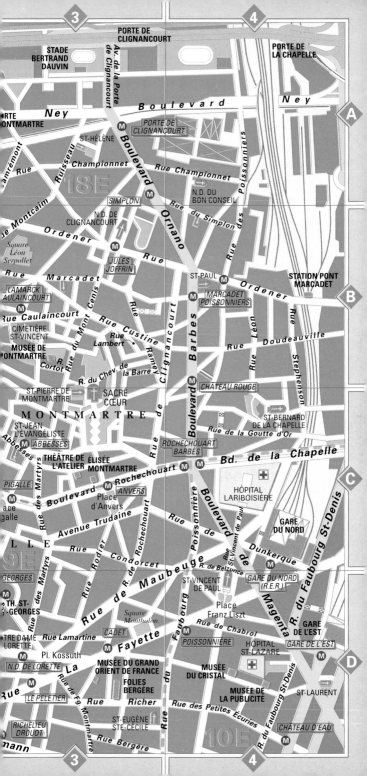

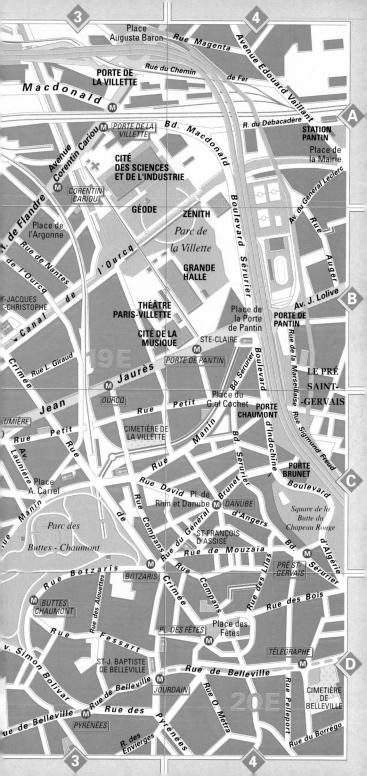

D

1 **2**

Foch

Place du M.al
de Lattre
de Tassigny

MUSÉE ARMÉNIEN
MUSÉE D'ENNERY

Route de
Suresnes

PORTE DAUPHINE Ⓜ

Avenue Bugeaud

Av. Victor Hug

A

STATION FOCH
PORTE DAUPHINE
(R.E.R.)

Rue des Belles Feuilles

Ⓜ *VICTOR HUGO*

MUSÉE DE LA
CONTREFAÇON

ST-ALBERT
LE GRAND

Place
Victor Hugo

Rue Copernic

Rue Laurist

UNIVERSITÉ
PARIS IX

ST-HONORÉ
D'EYLAU

NOUVELLE ÉGLISE
ST-HONORÉ D'EYLAU

Rue Kleb

Boulevard Lannes

Rue Flandrin

Rue de la Faisanderie

Rue Spontini

Rue de la Pompe

Avenue Victor Hugo

Rue Saint

Raymond Poincaré

Lauriston

R. L.
Delibes

Avenue

BOISSIÈR

Didier

Rue Dufrenoy

Rue de Longchamp

Place de
Mexico

Rue

Avenue d'Eylau

de

Villa d
Longcha

Longcham

STATION
H. MARTIN
(R.E.R.)

Avenue Victor Hugo

Ⓜ *POMPE*

N.D. DE
CHALDÉE

TROCADÉRO

Place
Tattegrain

Av.

Henri Martin

Avenue Georges Mandel

Place du
Trocadéro
et du 11 Novembre

Ⓜ

Avenue d

B

Boulevard Émile

Rue Octave Feuillet

CŒUR
IMMACULÉ
DE MARIE

Rue de la Pompe

Rue de Cortambert

16E

CIMETIÈRE
DE PASSY

ANNONCIATION

*Jardins du
Trocadéro*

Rue Franklin

PALAIS DE
CHAILLOT

Place d
Varsovi

Augier

Avenue Paul Doumer

Rue de la Tour

Av. des

Avenue

PON
D'IÉN

STATION
PASSY
LA MUETTE

MUETTE Ⓜ

Rue Nicolo

Rue Massenet

Rue de Passy

Place de
Costa Rica

MUSÉE
DU VIN

CHAMP DE MAR
(R.E.R.)

Av. Mozart

ⓂR. Bois le Vent

BOULAINVILLIERS (R.E.R.)

Rue

Rue Singer

N.D. DE
GRÂCE
DE PASSY

Rue Raynouard

PASSY Ⓜ

Quai

Ⓜ

Rue des Vignes

Place
Chopin

C

Ⓜ *RANELAGH*

Rue du Ranelagh

Rue de Boulainvilliers

Rue de Lamballe

Av. de Lamballe

PONT DE
BIR HAKEIM

BIR HAKEI

Rue de l'Assomption

AV. DU PRES. KENNEDY
MAISON DE RADIO-
FRANCE

Allée des Cygnes

Avenue du Président Kennedy

Ⓜ

Boulevar

Place
Rodin

(R.E.R.)

MAISON DE
RADIO-
FRANCE

Avenue de Grenelle

D

Rue La Fontaine

Rue Théophile Gautier

Rue Félicien David

Avenue de Versailles

PONT DE
GRENELLE

Quai de Grenelle

Rue Émeriau

Rue Charles

STATUE
DE LA LIBERTÉ

André Citroën

Rue Linois

Rue St-

Place
St-Charles

Rue Rouelle

Rue de Tourn

ST-TRINITÉ

Place de
Barcelone

15E

Place
Ch. Michels

Émile Zola

Place
du

MIRABEAU Ⓜ

*JAVEL
(R.E.R.)*

Av.

PONT
MIRABEAU

Ⓜ *JAVEL*

Avenue

de Javel

*CHARLES
MICHELS*

Place
Violet

1:17000

Quai

Rond Point du
Pt. Mirabeau

Rue

0   170   340 m

ST-CHRISTOPHE
DE JAVEL

1 **2**

E

CHAPELLE
EXPIATOIRE

GALERIES
LAFAYETTE

HAVRE CAUMARTIN
(R.E.R.)

Boulevard

ST-ESPRIT

Bd. Malesherbes

Rue Auber

OPÉRA

CHAUSSÉE
D'ANTIN

ARCHEVÊCHÉ
DE PARIS

R. Pasquier

R. de l'Arcade

Rue Tronchet

AUBER
(R.E.R.)

Rue Vignon

Place de
l'Opéra

QUAT
SEPTEM

Rue
du Faubourg St-Honoré

Place
Beauvau

A.

TH.
ÉDOUARD VII

A

Rue

TH. DE LA
MADELEINE

Place de la
Madeleine

OLYMPIA

Bd. des Capucines

OPÉRA

B

PALAIS DE
L'ÉLYSÉE

STE-MARIE
MADELEIN

Bd. de la
Madeleine

MADELEINE

R. Cambon

Rue des
Capucines

R. de la P

TH.
DANOU

TH. DE LA
POTINIER

Pl.
Gaillon

Avenue de l'Opéra

Avenue Gabriel

Rue Royale

R. Duphot

N.D. DE
L'ASSOMPTION

PLACE
VENDÔME

Pl. du
Marché
St-Honoré

St-Honoré

C.

Av. des
Champs Élysées

Rue Boissy d'Anglas

R. du Mont

Rue de Castiglione

R. de Thabor

PYRAMIDES

ST-ROCH

Vil

PETIT
PALAIS

CONCORDE

Rue
de

Rivoli

Place des
Pyramides

Av. Dutuit

Place de
la Concorde

JEU DE
PAUME

MUSÉE
DES ARTS
DÉCORATIFS

PALAIS ROY.

Cours la Reine

ORANGERIE

Jardin

TUILERIES

B

Quai
d'Orsay

PONT DE LA
CONCORDE

Quai des
Tuileries

des Tuileries

Jardin du

Seine

ARC DE TRIOMPHE
DU CARROUSEL

MUSÉE
LOUVR

INVALIDES
(R.E.R.)

PALAIS
BOURBON

Quai Anatole

Bd. St-Germain

MUSÉE
D'ORSAY
(R.E.R.)

PONT
SOLFÉRINO

Carrousel

ASSEMBLÉE
NATIONALE

France

PONT
ROYAL

Quai

INSTITUT
GÉOGRAPHIQUE
NATIONAL

MINISTÈRE DE
LA DÉFENSE

PALAIS DE
LA LÉGION
D'HONNEUR

MUSÉE
D'ORSAY

PONT DU
CARROUSEL

du

Rue
de

Rue de
Bac

R.

Quai Voltaire

Quai
Malaquais

F
l'Ins

SOLFÉRINO

Rue de Lille

Rue de Verneuil

INST
DE FRA

MINISTÈRE
DU TRAVAIL

STE-CLOTILDE

Boulevard

Rue de Bellechasse

de l'Université

R.
Beaux

VARENNE

Rue de Grenelle

PENTEMONT

MINISTÈRE
DES TRANSPORTS

Rue
Montalembert

ÉCOLE DES
BEAUX ARTS

Rue

Rue Jacol

MUSÉE
RODIN

RUE DU BAC

MUSÉE
DINA VIERNY

ST-THOMAS
D'AQUIN

UNIVERSITÉ
PARIS V

Saint-Germain

ST-GERMAIN
DES PRÉS

Ru
l'A

C

Boulevard des Invalides

Rue Vaneau

Rue
de

Varenne

Rue
du Bac

Rue de la
Chaise

ST-GERMAIN
DES PRÉS

HÔTEL
MATIGNON

Rue Récamier

Rue du

Four

MABIL

Rue de Babylone

Rue des
Canettes

R. Prin

ST-FRANÇOIS
XAVIER

SÈVRES BABYLONE

ST-SULPICE

Place
St-Sulpice

ST-SULPI

Bd. des Invalides

Rue Oudinot

Rue Vaneau

HÔPITAL
LAENNEC

Rue de Sèvres

ST-IGNACE

R. Dupin

Rue du Midi

Raspail

Rennes

Rue Madame

ST-JOSEPH
DES CARMES

Vaugirard

PALAI
LUXEMBO
(SE

CLINIQUE
ST-JEAN
DE DIEU

VANEAU

RENNES

Rue du Cherche

Rue de l'Abbé Grégoire

de

Rue

D

DUROC

HÔPITAL
NECKER

MUSÉE
HÉBERT

ST-PLACIDE

R. de Fleurus

Rue d'Assas

Jardin du
Luxembou

1:17000

0   170   340 m

Rue de Vaugirard

N.D. DES CHAMPS

8E
1ER
7E
6E
15E

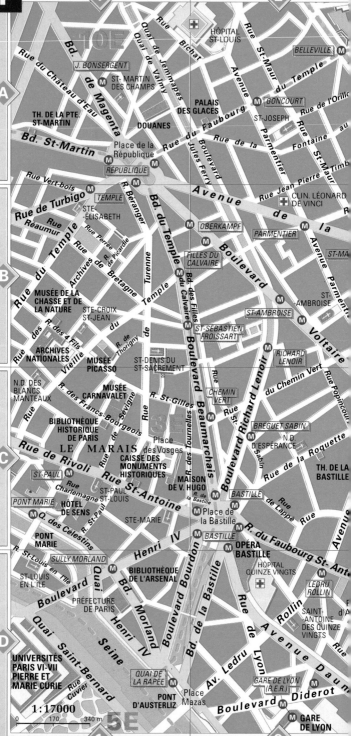

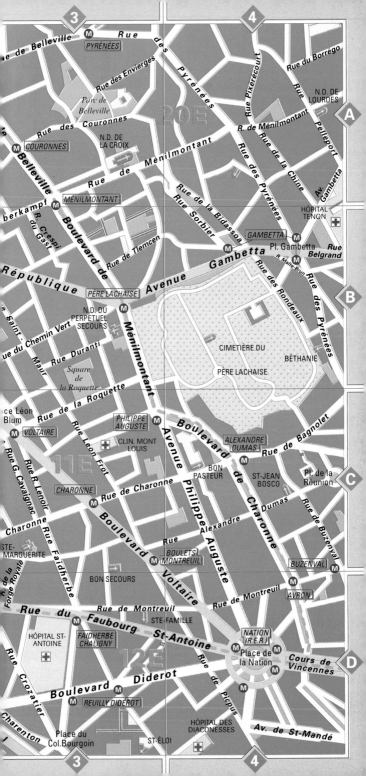

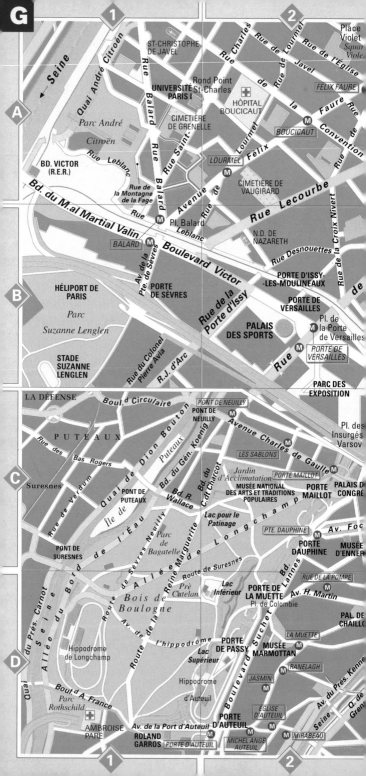

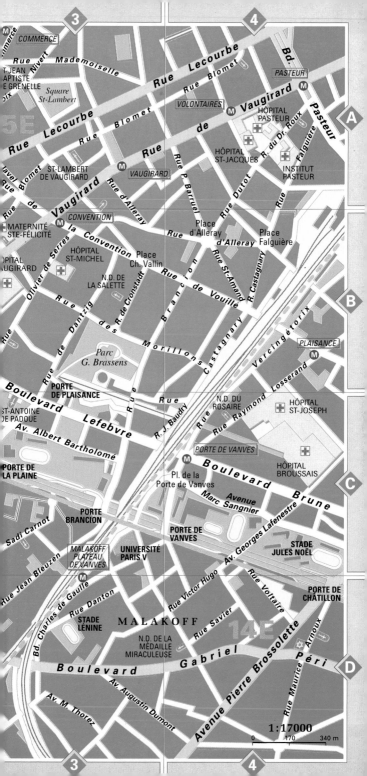

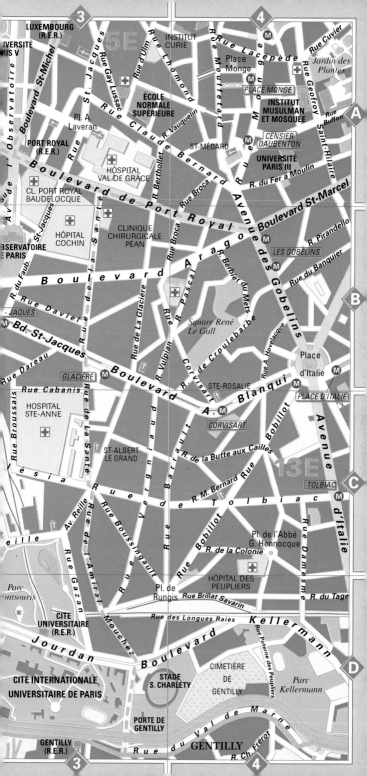

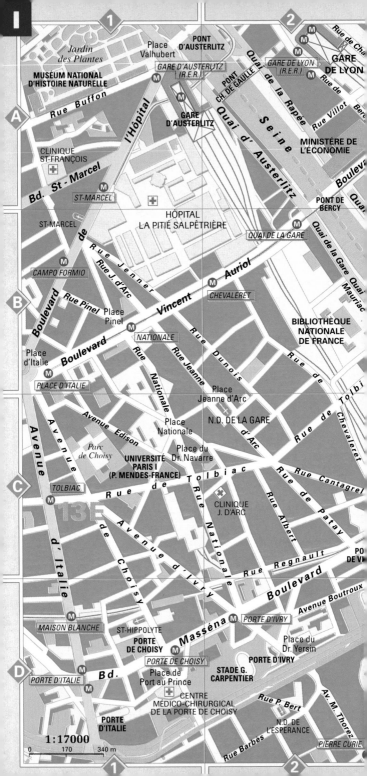

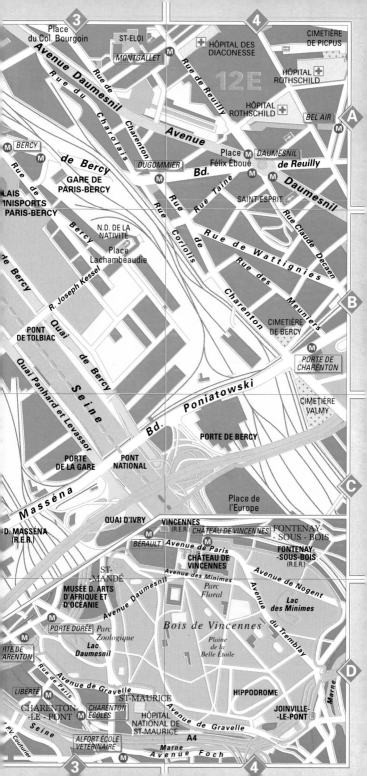

General Index
See pages 6 to 15 for practical
information and useful
telephone numbers.

Index

The publishers would like to thank
Eric Guillemot, Patrick Léger, Roger
Gain, Seymourina Cruse, Lionel
Monéger, and all the establishments
listed in this guide for their help.

Picture
Credits

01 *and cover illustration*
Denis Brumaud
6
CAV-J. M. Fabbro
8
Kristof Chemineau
(illustrations)
9
Kristof Chemineau
(illustrations),
Aéroports de Paris
(ADP logo)
10
Gallimard-Léonard
de Selva (stations),
CAV-J. M. Fabbro (TGV),
Thalys-SNCF CAV-J. J.
d'Angelo (Thalys logo),
Eurostar (Eurostar logo)
11
Gallimard-Patrick Léger
*(boulevard Saint-
Germain sign,
pedestrian signals,
parking meter,
parking sign)*,
Gallimard-Xavier Richer
(towing sign),
Gallimard-Lionel
Monéger *(pont Charles
de Gaulle sign)*
12
Didier Lauret
(métro, destination sign),
Gallimard-E. Guillemot
(bus sign),
RATP com/Audiovisuel-
Chabrol *(métro)*,
RATP-Thibaut *(logo)*,
RATP-Marguerite
(métro tickets)
13
Didier Lauret *(bus,
bus route, taxis stand,
Parisian taxi)*,
Gallimard-Patrick Léger
*(Batobus sign, métro
entrance)*,
RATP com/Audiovisuel-
Minoli *(Saint-Georges
sign)*
14
Gallimard-Éric Guillemot
(tickets, newspapers),
Gallimard-Xavier Richer
(police, call box),
Gallimard-Patrick Léger
*(letterbox, advertising
pillar, coins)*
15
France Télécom *(mobile
telephone)*,
Gallimard-Xavier Richer

(signs),
Gallimard-Patrick Léger
*(church, mosque,
synagogue)*,
DR *(phone card)*
16
Plaza Athénée
19
2 Gallimard-Patrick
Léger,
4 Hôtel Raphaël,
5 Gallimard-Patrick
Léger,
6 Hôtel Élysée Ceramic
21
7 Hôtel Baltimore,
8 Hôtel Le Parc
Victor Hugo,
9 K. Palace,
11 Hôtel Garden Élysées
23
12 Hôtel Vigny,
13 Hôtel Vernet,
14 Plaza Athénée,
15 San Régis
25
18 Le Crillon,
19 Marianne Haas,
21 Hôtel Meurice,
23 Royal St-Honoré
27
24 Concortel,
25 Westin Demeure
Hôtel Astor,
26 Hôtel Beau Manoir
29
29 Ritz,
30 C. Erwin,
31 Westminster
31
33 Gallimard-Patrick
Léger *(tiled wall)*,
33 Gallimard-Éric
Guillemot
(clocks),
36 Hôtel de la place
du Louvre
37 Gallimard-Patrick
Léger
33
40 Pavillon Bastille,
42 Hôtel du Jeu de
Paume *(interiors)*,
42 Brice Laval
(breakfast),
43 Hôtel Saint-Merry,
44 Hôtel Saint-Paul-
le-Marais
35
46 Relais Hôtel
Vieux Paris,
47 Hôtel Esméralda,
48 Relais Médicis,

49 Select Hôtel
(breakfast tray),
49 H.A. Ségalen
(atrium),
50 Les Rives de
Notre-Dame
37
52 Hôtel des Jardins
du Luxembourg,
53 Hôtel des Grands
Hommes,
55 Hôtel des Grandes
Écoles,
56 Le Clos Médicis
39
58 Relais Christine,
60 Gallimard-Patrick
Léger,
61 Buci Latin
41
62 Hôtel Montalembert,
63 Hôtel d'Angleterre,
65 Gallimard-Patrick
Léger
43
68 Hôtel Duc
de Saint-Simon,
69 Hôtel Lutétia,
71 Hôtel des
Saints-Pères
45
74 Hôtel Sainte-Beuve,
75 L'Atelier
Montparnasse,
76 Hôtel Raspail-
Montparnasse
46
Le Grand Véfour
49
1 P. Mauver,
2 Gallimard-Patrick
Léger,
3 Marot-Gaudry,
4 Gallimard-Patrick
Léger,
5 La Samaritaine,
6 Gallimard-Roger Gain
53
9 Guy Savoy
(plate, kitchen),
9 Gallimard-Roger
Gain *(interior)*,
10 Taira,
12 F. Rambert
55
15 J. Bourboulon et
Gallimard-Roger Gain
(interior),
17 Gallimard-Patrick
Léger
18 Le Petit Colombier
57
22 Alain Ducasse
(façade),
22 Gallimard-Gérard
Nencioli *(plate)*,
22 DR *(bar)*,
25 Faugeron
59
Gallimard-Patrick Léger,
26 Yachts de Paris,
28 Gallimard-
Patrick Léger,
29 Café Six-Huit
61
33 Laurent,

34 Pavillon
Ledoyen *(façade)*,
34 Gallimard-Roger
Gain *(terrace)*,
35 Gallimard-
Roger Gain
63
36 Lucas Carton,
38 Le Carré des
Feuillants,
40 Gallimard-
Roger Gain,
41 Gallimard-
Gérard Nencioli
65
42 L'Œnothèque,
43 Casa Olympe,
44 Guilhaume-
Saint-Amour,
45 Drouant *(staircase)*,
45 Gallimard-Gérard
Nencioli *(Salon
Goncourt, sign)*
66
47 Gallimard-
Roger Gain,
48 Maxim's
(Sem drawing),
48 Gallimard-Roger
Gain *(façade)*,
50 Gallimard-Roger
Gain,
53 Gallimard-
Roger Gain
67
49 Gallimard-
Roger Gain,
50 Gallimard-
Roger Gain,
51 Gallimard-
Roger Gain,
53 Gallimard-Gérard
Nencioli *(ceiling
paintings)*,
53 Gallimard-
Roger Gain
(room)
69
55 Gallimard-
Roger Gain,
56 Table d'Anvers
71
60 Le Grand Véfour
(plate),
60 Gallimard-
Roger Gain *(room)*,
61 Gérard Besson,
62 Café Marly
73
66 Miraville,
67 Le Monde
des Chimères,
68 Gallimard-
Roger Gain,
69 Bofinger *(dome)*,
69 Gallimard-Roger
Gain *(panel, roses)*
74
73 Gallimard-
Roger Gain,
74 Gallimard-
Gilbert Nencioli,
75 Gallimard-
Roger Gain,
76 Gallimard-
Gilbert Nencioli